A Secondary Religious Education Course
Book 2

The Kingdom of Heaven

Richard Hughes

Oxford

A note to the teacher

Religious Education in schools needs to pick itself up by its bootlaces. An improvement in teaching will lead to an improvement in status and vice versa. But the process must begin somewhere. One of the ways in which the situation can be remedied is by supplying non-specialist teachers with carefully-planned textbooks. That is the purpose of this present book. If RE is to be useful within the general curriculum of the school, its presentation requires a degree of sophistication. The problems of the Reformation, for instance, cannot be explained by telling the children Bible stories. Religious ideas have changed and developed over the centuries and, right from the beginning, pupils need to be aware that such changes have taken place. In this book, pupils are shown that the teachings of Jesus of Nazareth were delivered in criticism of his own religious background and that there have been many differing interpretations of his ideas since his time. That explains the pattern of this book. Each group of lessons begins with Jesus' teaching on a particular topic. The topic is then shown in a series of different contexts illustrating both the background to his ideas and the ways in which his ideas were interpreted at different times. At the end of the first year, pupils will not, of course, be able to understand the various theological arguments which took place at the Reformation but, in that they will have been given the right terms of reference, a start will have been made. Subjects like history, English literature and RE do not converge until fifth and sixth form level but the spadework has to be done lower down the school.

One of the characteristics of religion, though, is that it expresses itself in many different literary genres. The Bible, for example, is a library of law books, history (or quasi-history) books, wisdom literature, legend, fiction, poetry and prophecy, to say nothing of gospels and letters. It seems only fair to attempt to reflect this in the pattern of the lessons. The Jesus story at the beginning of each group of lessons has been adapted from the New Testament using modern literary technique. New Testament writers, in accordance with the writing conventions of the time, never thought of telling the reader what the surroundings were like or in what tone of voice people spoke. In that sense, there is an imaginative element to the stories although the actual account sticks as closely as possible to the New Testament. The second and fourth lessons in each group are, as far as possible, straightforwardly factual and historical, showing the impact of religious ideas on people and events. In contrast, the third lesson is meant to widen the discussion imaginatively in some way or other. A piece of evocative fiction or some kind of broad discussion of the topic can be an effective way of shedding new light on religious ideas. The final lesson in each group is a summary lesson, showing contemporary Christian ideas in relation to the topic.

Although the book has been organised in groups of five lessons, each lesson is complete in itself and occupies a spread – two face-to-face pages which, when opened, present everything required for that lesson. The text, illustrations and questions on each spread will supply enough material to keep a class fully occupied for the duration of a thirty-five minute lesson. There is also a sixth spread with each group of lessons, supplying a variety of comprehension questions, questions requiring some research, and questions inviting the use of imagination. In schools where lessons are seventy minutes long, two lesson spreads can be used or one lesson spread followed by work on the questions. One of the aims of this textbook has been to see that pupils have an almost inexhaustible supply of things to do. The stories are large enough to stimulate the most able pupils while being simple enough to interest the less able. I make no apology for concentrating on Christianity in this book. It is, I believe, of great importance that all pupils, regardless of their own backgrounds should be able to understand the impact of Christianity on our culture.

Whitchurch on Thames   Richard Hughes

Contents

Cover illustration by Paul Leith

Oxford University Press, Walton Street, Oxford OX2 6DP

Oxford London Glasgow
New York Toronto Melbourne Auckland
Kuala Lumpur Singapore Hong Kong Tokyo
Delhi Bombay Calcutta Madras Karachi
Nairobi Dar es Salaam Cape Town

and associated companies in
Beirut Berlin Ibadan Mexico City Nicosia

OXFORD is a trade mark of Oxford University Press

© Richard Hughes 1982
First Published 1982
Reprinted 1983
ISBN 0 19 918135 7

Phototypeset by Tradespools Limited, Frome, Somerset
Printed in Hong Kong

Jesus describes God's generosity

Jesus was brought up in Nazareth, a remote, ancient village on a hillside above a high valley. But when he began his ministry, he centred his life not on Nazareth but on Capernaum, one of the coastal towns of the Sea of Galilee. The contrast could not have been greater. Capernaum was a busy centre of commerce. There was a large fountain on the edge of the town which was used to irrigate the prosperous farms in the vicinity. The businessmen of the town itself were mostly concerned with the catching and marketing of fish. Jesus' earliest disciples belonged to this fishing community of Capernaum. Peter, for instance, was a married man and owned a boat. Jesus regularly stayed at his house. The town was important enough to have a small Roman garrison and it had the largest synagogue in Israel at the time. The local Roman centurion had surprised people by contributing to the cost of this building.

But while the place had an air of prosperity, the contrast between rich and poor was much in evidence. The poverty of Israel as a whole is indicated by the emigration figures of the time. While there were half a million Jews living in Palestine, four million lived abroad. Seven out of every eight Jews found it easier to make a living elsewhere. And the demands of Rome added to the burden. Galilee and Peraea (the desert area beyond the Jordan) paid a tribute to the Romans of two million denarii a year. This was a considerable sum.

Capernaum as it is today

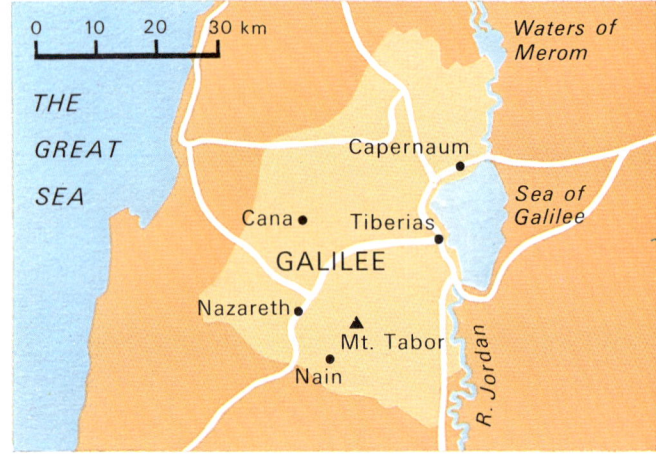

Galilee

A denarius was the amount of money which it was reckoned a labourer should earn in a day. So while the merchants, farmers and fishermen of Capernaum were well off, there were many other people who had a minimum of food and clothing. There was a great deal of unemployment. One of Jesus' stories is about the men who stood around the market place all day hoping that someone would give them work. Tax gatherers collected money from rich and poor alike. The taxes often plunged poor people into debt.

There were two sets of laws which could be applied to debtors in first-century Palestine. In Jewish law, a debtor was held in slavery for six years by the person to whom he owed money. Jewish law also said that a man should treat his slaves with kindness. Under Roman law, however, debtors were often imprisoned and tortured. Usually, Jews and Romans followed their own laws but Herod Antipas, the Jewish ruler of Galilee, scandalized the people of his time by treating debtors according to Roman law. He imprisoned them in the gloomy fortress of the Machaerus on the east bank of the Dead Sea.

Denarius from Jesus' time

wept and fell down on his knees before the treasurer. But the treasurer would not listen. He immediately ordered imprisonment and torture.' Jesus' hearers were full of indignation at the thought of it. 'But when the king heard,' said Jesus, 'he was furious. He sent out his guard to arrest the crooked treasurer and he never saw the outside of a prison again.' So far as Jesus's audience was concerned, it was a fitting end to the story. 'In the same way,' continued Jesus, 'God will punish everyone who does not forgive his brothers.'

With that parting sentence, Jesus transformed his story. He was no longer talking about money but about religion. Every human being owed a vast, unpayable debt to God. God, in his generosity, had given the sky, the sea, the fields and the mountains. God had given life itself. No fortune, however great, could be worth as much. And human beings treated God's possessions as if they were their own. But what made God angry was human meanness. Just as the treasurer had delivered his fellow countryman to the torturers for a sum a million times less than he himself owed, so human beings forgot God's generosity as they ill-treated each other. Jesus' story about the eccentric owner of the vineyard makes the same point. God gives his good gifts to people whether they deserve them or not, but human beings squabble and some think they deserve more than others.

It was the poorer sorts of people who took most notice of Jesus' teachings, but he did not particularly wish his followers to be poor. He taught only that the quest for God was more important than the acquisition of wealth. For that reason, Peter, Andrew, James and John left their boats and their homes and followed Jesus the length and breadth of Palestine.

One of Jesus' favourite methods was to tell a story which described a fantastical situation. He told, for instance, how the men in the market place were employed by the eccentric owner of a vineyard. Some of the men worked for twelve hours, others for six and others for only one. Yet, at the end of the day, the employer insisted on paying everybody a full day's wage – a denarius. It caused a terrible row. Another of Jesus' stories was about people in debt. 'There was once', he said, 'a king's treasurer who cheated his master of a hundred million denarii.' It was an astonishing beginning to a story. The man owed fifty times the annual tribute to Rome! 'So the king', said Jesus, 'ordered that he, his wife and his children should become slaves. But the treasurer wept and fell down on his knees before the king. And the king was so moved by what he said that he forgave him the whole debt.' To the subjects of Herod Antipas, the king's behaviour was almost as incredible as the debt itself.

'Some time later,' said Jesus, 'the treasurer came across a fellow countryman who owed him a hundred denarii. He took him violently by the throat and demanded instant payment. The man

Understand your work

1 What was life like in first century Capernaum?

2 Which law did the king use when first dealing with the treasurer and which did he finally use?

3 In what ways did Jesus compare human beings to the crooked treasurer?

2 The psalmist admires the world

In his story of the great debt, Jesus compared God's generosity with the way in which human beings treat each other. Centuries earlier, a Hebrew psalmist came across an ancient Egyptian hymn to the disc of the sun. He adapted it so that its meaning could be applied to the God of Israel. It shows how the landscape reflects God's power and goodness.

PSALM 104

PRAISE the Lord, O my soul: O Lord my God, thou art become exceeding glorious; thou art clothed with majesty and honour.

2 Thou deckest thyself with light as it were with a garment: and spreadest out the heavens like a curtain.

3 Who layeth the beams of his chambers in the waters: and maketh the clouds his chariot, and walketh upon the wings of the wind.

4 He maketh his angels spirits: and his ministers a flaming fire.

5 He laid the foundations of the earth: that it never should move at any time.

6 Thou coveredst it with the deep like as with a garment: the waters stand in the hills.

7 At thy rebuke they flee: at the voice of thy thunder they are afraid.

8 They go up as high as the hills, and down to the valleys beneath: even unto the place which thou hast appointed for them.

9 Thou hast set them their bounds which they shall not pass: neither turn again to cover the earth.

10 He sendeth the springs into the rivers: which run among the hills.

11 All beasts of the field drink thereof: and the wild asses quench their thirst.

12 Beside them shall the fowls of the air have their habitation: and sing among the branches.

13 He watereth the hills from above: the earth is filled with the fruit of thy works.

14 He bringeth forth grass for the cattle: and green herb for the service of men;

15 That he may bring food out of the earth, and wine that maketh glad the heart of man: and oil to make him a cheerful countenance, and bread to strengthen man's heart.

16 The trees of the Lord also are full of sap: even the cedars of Libanus which he hath planted;

17 Wherein the birds make their nests: and the fir-trees are a dwelling for the stork.

18 The high hills are a refuge for the wild goats: and so are the stony rocks for the conies.

19 He appointed the moon for certain seasons: and the sun knoweth his going down.

20 Thou makest darkness that it may be night: wherein all the beasts of the forest do move.

21 The lions roaring after their prey: do seek their meat from God.

22 The sun ariseth, and they get them away together: and lay them down in their dens.

23 Man goeth forth to his work, and to his labour: until the evening.

24 O Lord, how manifold are thy works: in wisdom hast thou made them all; the earth is full of thy riches.

25 So is the great and wide sea also: wherein are things creeping innumerable, both small and great beasts.

26 There go the ships, and there is that Leviathan: whom thou hast made to take his pastime therein.

27 These wait all upon thee: that thou mayest give them meat in due season.

28 When thou givest it them they gather it: and when thou openest thy hand they are filled with good.

29 When thou hidest thy face they are troubled: when thou takest away their breath they die, and are turned again to their dust.

30 When thou lettest thy breath go forth they shall be made: and thou shalt renew the face of the earth.

31 The glorious Majesty of the Lord shall endure for ever: the Lord shall rejoice in his works.

32 The earth shall tremble at the look of him: if he do but touch the hills, they shall smoke.

33 I will sing unto the Lord as long as I live: I will praise my God while I have my being.

34 And so shall my words please him: my joy shall be in the Lord.

35 As for sinners, they shall be consumed out of the earth, and the ungodly shall come to an end: praise thou the Lord, O my soul, praise the Lord.

Understand your work

1 At the time when the psalm was written, people believed that the sea was much higher than the land. (You can see why if you stand on a beach and look at the horizon.) What explanation does the psalmist give for the fact that the landscape is not flooded?

2 The psalmist appreciated simple commodities like oil, wine and bread. What does he say about them?

3 What does the psalmist say about death and how does he react to the idea that, one day, he himself is going to die?

9

Christmas with a car

'Overwork,' the doctor had said. 'He needs a complete and long rest.' So that summer, John Williams had resigned his post as vicar of a large industrial parish. He and his wife, Belinda, had moved out of the eight-bedroomed vicarage into a small rented cottage in a Cotswold village. John and Belinda had three sons and two daughters, all teenagers. At the cottage, they seemed to fill every corner. They played loud pop music, used sewing machines and electric drills and generally created pandemonium. Fortunately, during the week they were at school. So was Belinda who was a teacher. It was the time that they were out of the cottage which gave John the rest he needed. He felt useless; wretched. The man who had worked so hard for so long was suffering a violent reaction. He didn't want to go anywhere or see anybody. He was all wrapped up in himself.

'As soon as school breaks up,' said Belinda about a month before Christmas, 'we can all go to Ffestiniog.' It was an excellent idea. A friend of the family had a large house in Wales which they could borrow. So the plans were made. Nobody would enjoy Christmas cramped up in the cottage and it didn't matter where an unemployed ex-vicar spent the holiday. Then, the day before the family was due to leave, John went over to the village shop for a loaf. 'Have you heard the news?' said the shopkeeper. 'Our rector has had a heart attack! They've taken him to hospital.' John rushed to the hospital to see him. He was gravely ill. 'Is there anything I can do?' he asked the rector's wife who was staying at her husband's bedside. 'Could you cope with Christmas services?' she asked. 'Certainly,' said John and went home to explain to Belinda. 'You take everybody to Wales,' he said, 'and I will come on Christmas Day when the services are over.'

The family, including the cat, departed the following day in Belinda's estate car. John was left with a quiet cottage and an ancient car which belonged to his father. In the days that followed, he was extremely busy. He visited the rector every day, said prayers with him and watched his gradual recovery. He supervised the decorating of the church, attended choir practice, held a meeting of the bellringers and gave communion to an elderly couple who were both bedridden. On Christmas Eve, he was standing in the bathroom, razor in hand, his face covered in lather. Suddenly he stared at himself in the mirror. He felt better than he had felt for months! He realized that he had stopped thinking about himself.

There was ice on the road as John drove up to the church. He felt remarkably cheerful. The church bells were ringing. He had spoken to Belinda on the phone. Even the old car seemed to be going well. At half-past eleven, the service began. 'See, amid the winter snow . . .' sang the choristers as the crucifer led them in procession. John followed, admiring the red cassocks and the crisp white surplices which contrasted with the dark clothes of the congregation. The Christmas tree supplied a warm glow to the ancient church and the candles

sparkled against the background of the stone reredos. The church was crowded. As he passed into the sanctuary, John glanced at the crib, a little pool of light in which could be seen the delicate figures of Joseph, Mary and child, surrounded by shepherds and animals. This was the way to celebrate the birth of the Christ-child.

It was two o'clock in the morning when John finally got to bed. After the service he had been invited to sherry by some people who lived near the church. He was up again at seven – only five hours sleep but he didn't mind. At half-past seven he was back in church getting ready for the eight o'clock communion service. At nine, he held another communion service at a daughter church a few miles away. Then he came back for his final Christmas service at eleven. This was not communion but Morning Prayer, and many of the people who had attended on Christmas Eve came

again. The church was crowded once more, and afterwards people stayed behind to wish each other 'happy Christmasses'. Before he set off for Wales, John was invited to the house of an elderly parishioner. She gave him a glass of champagne and a smoked-salmon sandwich.

John hoped the journey would go well. It didn't. He had done ten out of the hundred and sixty miles when two things happened simultaneously. It began to snow and the radiator of the ancient car began to boil. The cylinder-head gasket had blown and the only way he would get to Wales would be by putting water in the radiator every few miles. If he hadn't been so tired, John would have found it funny. As the snow thickened, the car was sliding around while great clouds of steam rose out of the engine. It was more like a 'puffing billy' than a car. There were no other cars on the road and no garages open. John found an old oil can and filled it with water every time he came across a tap. The journey which normally took four and a half hours dragged on and on. He had left at one, and by five o'clock he was half-way. Then he had a puncture in a back wheel. John looked at it despondently. The tyre was a good one and there was no sensible explanation – just bad luck. He took the jack out of the boot. It was frozen and would not move. . . .

At eleven o'clock in the evening of that Christmas Day, the ancient car puffed up the last few hundred yards to the house where the family was staying. The teenagers rushed to meet him, throwing snowballs and whooping. Suddenly, John felt a surge of gratefulness. He had made it. God had been good to him. God had given him an impossible, overworked and underfed Christmas to cure him from feeling sorry for himself. It gave him great confidence.

Understand your work

1 What are the following objects: cassock, surplice, reredos? What is a crucifer?

2 How did John feel at the beginning of the communion service on Christmas Eve?

3 What went wrong during John's journey?

The sermon preached at the Spittle

London at the end of the sixteenth century

Trinity House on the Thames in the sixteenth century was responsible for such activities as the care of beacons and buoys in the river, the training of river pilots, and the control of the design and construction of ships for the navy. In the event of war, Trinity House superintended the defence of London. Such, then, were the responsibilities of people like Thomas Andrewes who was one of the masters of Trinity House. He was married with thirteen children, the eldest being Lancelot who had been born in 1555. The boy grew up well acquainted with the comings and goings of the Port of London. He was a clever boy and, at the age of ten, he became a pupil at the famous Merchant Taylors' School, under the headmastership of Richard Mulcaster. Mulcaster was one of the leading educationalists of the time and had made a name for himself by devising the pageantry when the young Elizabeth first rode into London to be made Queen. At the age of sixteen, Lancelot Andrewes moved on to Pembroke Hall, Cambridge. While he was there, he became a clergyman and, eventually, rose to be Master of his college.

Although Lancelot Andrewes remained in Cambridge until he was thirty-three years old, he did not lose contact with the way of life which he had known in his childhood. Twice or three times a year, he walked from Cambridge to London and spent several weeks staying with his parents. He was enthusiastic about learning foreign languages and, during his visits to London, he made a point of taking lessons from some of the foreigners who lived near the port.

In Elizabethan times, it was usual in the city of London to hold processions on certain holy days to one or other of the pulpit crosses. On the Wednesday after Easter each year, for instance, the Lord Mayor and Aldermen of the city, dressed in their finery, together with the Bishop and leading clergymen, used to accompany the rich merchants of the Port of London on a procession to the pulpit cross of St. Mary's Hospital. The procession started at the port and wound its way through the streets to the grounds of the ancient priory where the pulpit cross stood. The procession ended with a sermon. The pulpit was a dovecote-like structure in which the preacher stood and on top of which was the cross. The merchants stood in the open spaces around the pulpit while an open-fronted two-storey building acted as a grandstand for the Lord Mayor and the visiting dignitaries.

In 1588, while he was still at Cambridge, Lancelot Andrewes was invited to preach at the pulpit cross of the priory of St. Mary's Hospital on the Wednesday after Easter. The word 'hospital' had been shortened to 'Spittle' or 'Spital' and he was to be the preacher 'at the Spittle'. It was a great civic occasion. People lined the route, waving and cheering as the carriages and the marchers passed. The site of the pulpit cross, however, was not as grand in 1588 as it had been in the past. The priory had been dissolved by Henry VIII and the old building was empty and crumbling. Most of the grounds had been sold off and the graveyard of the priory was used for artillery practice. Only the pulpit cross itself remained unscathed with the passage of time.

Although Lancelot Andrewes had been a clergyman for a long time, this was his first important sermon. It must have been quite an ordeal for this quiet university lecturer to find himself at the centre of a grand London procession. When everybody had assembled, he climbed into the pulpit and began with his text from the first letter to Timothy: 'Charge them that be rich in this world, that they be not high minded . . .' Andrewes' sermon lasted two and a half hours. He began by charging his audience not to use money for evil

purposes. He explained how well he knew the people of the Port of London:

> No where do they sucke the abundance of the Sea and the treasure hid in the sand, in like measure. No where are the Merchants noble-men's fellowes, and able to lend the Princes of the earth so much as here.

He reminded them that, without God's generosity, there would be no wealth for them or for anybody else. Then, half-way through his sermon, Andrewes changed the meaning of the word 'charge'. In his text, the word meant 'instruct' and Andrewes had been instructing his rich audience. But now Andrewes began actually charging his rich congregation money. There were many poor people in Elizabethan London. They needed food and clothing. Their children needed education. But there were no provisions for them in those days. It was quite possible for poor people to die of starvation. In the past, the monks had helped the poor but now the monasteries were closed. It was up to the rich merchants, of their generosity, to help. Andrewes was not expecting small sums of money. 'Men would be doing good too cheape,' he said. 'I know the charges will be great . . . but the good done will be so great.'

We are not told how Andrewes' audience reacted to his sermon. Many of them were probably not keen to give money away. Perhaps some of them heckled him. But Andrewes was following the example of Jesus. 'The Sermon preached at the Spittle' has a great deal in common with Jesus' story of the wicked treasurer. In both, human beings are encouraged to be as generous as God himself. And like the Hebrew psalmist, Andrewes saw God's gifts in the world around him: 'the abundance of the Sea and the treasure hid in the sand'. It was God, too, who had given the merchants the ability to make money. Confidence and ability, as John Williams found out, are also parts of God's generosity.

The year when Lancelot Andrewes preached at the Spittle is well remembered in English history. Later that year, the Spanish Armada appeared off the coast of Britain.

Understand your work

1 How did Lancelot Andrewes maintain contact with the Port of London after he had become a member of Pembroke Hall, Cambridge?

2 Why was it called 'The Sermon preached at the Spittle'?

3 What did Lancelot Andrewes talk about in his sermon?

13

5

Florence 1966

In the fourteenth and fifteenth centuries, the city of Florence was at the centre of a great artistic movement. Art flourished in a bewildering variety of forms. There were many influences. The relics of the classical sculptures of ancient Greece and Rome were still scattered in the Italian countryside. The teachings of the followers of St. Francis of Assisi, emphasizing God's love and generosity, gave the movement a strong religious background. There were also trade links with other Mediterranean civilizations. Against such a background, there came painters like Giotto to revolutionize the idea of art. Giotto studied the movements of people and animals. He was interested in the way in which trees grow and hills recede into the distance. He tried to make his paintings strong and simple. In 1334, Giotto was appointed town architect of Florence and parts of the cathedral are his work. And Giotto was followed by others. The sculptor Ghiberti, for instance, spent twenty-one years making a pair of fine doors depicting biblical scenes for the baptistry of the cathedral. He then spent the rest of his life making a second pair of doors.

Florence was soon a treasure house of paintings, sculptures and buildings. In the following century, the artists of Florence were encouraged and subsidized by a powerful noble family called Medici. The Medici palace was the artistic centre of the city. Under Cosimo de' Medici, an academy was set up for the study of Greek and Roman art. Talented people came from far and near. A great interest in science developed. The work was further encouraged by his grandson, Lorenzo de' Medici, who was himself a poet and a scholar. Michelangelo produced sculptures for the Medici chapel and Botticelli, during his time in Florence, produced delicate illustrations of Dante's poetry. But the interest in Greek and Roman mythology upset some of the preachers of the time, particularly Savonarola. He believed that such influences

Students and restoration experts working on damaged manuscripts after the flood

corrupted Christianity. He condemned the paintings of nymphs and mythical creatures and, towards the end of the century, he encouraged the people of Florence to burn a great many of the art treasures.

Apart from the problems posed by preachers like Savonarola, there has always been one great disadvantage to Florence as a city. The river Arno has overflowed into the city fifty-four times in the last six hundred years. The river wreaked destruction, for instance, in 1269, in 1288 and again in 1333. Giotto himself, then, must have been aware of the problem. It might not have seemed important in Giotto's time when the first art works were appearing in the city. But when the news broke that on the night of 3rd November 1966, the river had burst into the city yet again, engulfing everything in a sea of oil, water and mud, alarm was felt throughout the whole world. The treasures of Florence were irreplaceable.

The floods from the river swept along the streets of Florence at terrifying speeds. Cars and trees were smashed. Water burst into libraries, churches and art galleries alike. In the days that followed, Florence was a scene of great devastation. There were the bodies of seventy drowned horses at the race course. Documents and manuscripts of great rarity were floating in the waters which flowed through the Biblioteca Nazionale – the library. Cimabue's picture of the crucifixion in the church of Santa Croce had been destroyed. There was mutiny in the prison of Santa Teresa. Many

prisoners dived off the walls and some perished. Many of the paintings at the Uffizi Gallery would require expensive restoration. As the waters receded, they left a thick layer of mud. There seemed little hope of recovering the glories of Florence.

Amazingly, a visit to modern Florence shows little of the damage and devastation caused by the flood of 1966. Almost everything has been restored because the disaster roused the generosity of the world. The restoration of Florence is one of the miracle stories of the twentieth century. Art experts of all kinds poured into the city and gave their services free. Students laboured fourteen hours a day to clear mud and to salvage the books of the Biblioteca Nazionale. Young people and old, foreigners and Italians, priests and communists worked alongside each other. Money poured in from the most unexpected quarters. A few years earlier, a landslide from a coal tip had destroyed the village school in Aberfan in the South Wales valleys. Aberfan sent toys to the children of Florence.

When Jesus told his story of the dishonest treasurer, he was complaining of the meanness with which people treat each other compared to the generosity with which God treats them. Some of the people of Florence in 1966 also complained. 'There seems plenty of money for art treasures,' they said, 'but not much for helping the poor people of the city.' They were wrong. The art treasures bring the tourists to Florence and put money into the pockets of the people. As the psalmist understood a long time ago, human beings are enriched by their surroundings. The story of the restoration of Florence has the opposite message to Jesus' story of the dishonest treasurer. Jesus pointed out how mean people can be but the story of Florence shows how generous people can be. It was, of course, that kind of generosity that Jesus was trying to encourage in his followers. It was that kind of generosity, too, that Lancelot Andrewes was seeking from the rich merchants of sixteenth-century London. And, as John Williams discovered, experiences, evil in themselves, can sometimes bring out the best in people.

Understand your work

1 Why could the city of Florence be described as a treasure house of art?

2 What were the effects of the flood?

3 What has happened to Florence since the flood?

Work Section

Understand your work

1 What story did Jesus tell about unemployment in first-century Galilee?

2 How did Herod Antipas' behaviour scandalize the Jews of the time?

3 How does the psalmist describe God in Psalm 104?

4 What does the psalmist say about the behaviour of lions?

5 Why did John Williams resign as vicar of a large industrial parish?

6 Why did John Williams feel a lucky man when he finally arrived at Ffestiniog?

7 Describe the scene at the pulpit cross when Lancelot Andrewes preached.

8 How did Lancelot Andrewes describe the prosperity of the Port of London and how was that prosperity threatened?

9 What contribution did Giotto make to the development of Florence?

10 How did the world react to the flood in Florence?

Correct these statements

1 Herod Antipas insisted on paying everyone a denarius.

2 The crooked treasurer owed Jesus a large sum of money.

3 There was a ship in Old Testament times called Leviathan.

4 The psalmist was an Egyptian discus thrower.

5 John Williams ate nothing but smoked salmon and drank champagne.

6 John Williams made a cup of tea when his radiator boiled.

7 The Elizabethan merchants used Lancelot Andrewes for artillery practice.

8 In 'The Sermon preached at the Spittle', Lancelot Andrewes was trying to raise money for the priory.

9 Lorenzo de' Medici was very good at painting animals.

10 Savonarola dived off the walls of the prison into the flood.

Find out more

1 When the priests in exile in Babylon wrote their account of the Creation, they set it within the framework of a week. Read Genesis 1, 1–2, 3. What did God create on each day?
a Sunday
b Monday
c Tuesday
d Wednesday
e Thursday
f Friday
What did God do on Saturday?

2 When Moses led the children of Israel out of Egypt, he told them that they would be able to inhabit the promised land at the end of their journey. Read Deuteronomy 8, 7–10. What was the promised land like?

3 Moses also told them to thank God for the gifts of the promised land. Read Deuteronomy 26, 1–4. How were the Israelites to thank God?

4 At the beginning of St. Luke's Gospel, Mary rejoices to hear that she is to be Jesus' mother. Read Luke 1, 46–55 and answer the following questions:
a What is meant by the word 'magnify'?
b What does the phrase 'those who fear him' mean?
c How has God treated the proud and the mighty?
d What does Mary say about Israel?

5 In Lancelot Andrewes' time, the priory of St. Mary's Hospital had been dissolved but there were other 'hospitals' in the city of London. Find out about Christ's Hospital and answer the following questions:
a What is Christ's Hospital?
b Who preached the sermon that led to its founding?
c Who founded it?
d By whose generosity was it founded?
e Where was it originally?
f Where is it now?

6 Since the earliest times, Christians have celebrated the birth of Christ with a feast. Here is part of the Gloucester Wassail:

Wassail, wassail, all over the town!
Our toast it is white and our ale it is brown,
Our bowl it is made of the white maple tree,
With our wassail bowl we'll drink to thee.

So here is to Cherry and to his right cheek,
Pray God send our master a good piece of beef,
And a good piece of beef that may we all see;
With our wassail bowl we'll drink to thee.

And here's to Dobbin and to his right eye,
Pray God send our master a good Christmas pie,
And a good Christmas pie that may we all see;
With our wassail bowl we'll drink to thee.

So here's to Broad May and to her broad horn,
May God send our master a good crop of corn,
And a good crop of corn that may we all see;
With our wassail bowl we'll drink to thee.

And here's to Fillpail and to her left ear,
May God send our master a happy New Year,
And a happy New Year as e'er he did see;
With our wassail bowl we'll drink to thee.

Answer the following questions:

a Two horses and two cows are mentioned in the carol. What are the names of the cows?

b What gives the impression that this was a carol for farm labourers?

c Make a list of the things they wanted for their master.

d Why was their master's prosperity so important?

7 Describe your own experience of Christmas.

8 Gerard Manley Hopkins, a Roman Catholic priest, celebrated God's generosity in many of his poems. Here is one of them:

Pied Beauty

Glory be to God for dappled things –
For skies of couple-colour as a brinded cow;
For rose-moles all in stipple upon trout that swim;
Fresh-firecoal chestnut-falls; finches' wings;
Landscape plotted and pieced – fold, fallow and
plough;
And all trades, their gear and tackle and trim.

All things counter, original, spare, strange;
Whatever is fickle, freckled (who knows how?)
With swift, slow; sweet, sour, adazzle, dim;
He fathers-forth whose beauty is past change:
Praise him.

Answer the following questions:

a What kind of skies does Hopkins admire?

b What does he like about the trout?

c What does he mean by 'Landscape plotted and pieced'?

d Why does he say that God's beauty is past change?

9 Find and copy into your exercise book the General Thanksgiving from the Book of Common Prayer.

10 Every year, on the Sunday nearest 11th November, these words are said:

They shall grow not old as we that are left grow old:
Age shall not weary them, nor the years condemn.
At the going down of the sun and in the morning
We will remember them.

Answer the following questions:

a What is the Sunday called?

b Why do people thank God on that Sunday?

c Who are the people who will not grow old?

d What is the symbol of that Sunday?

Use your imagination

1 Describe Jesus' story of the crooked treasurer from the point of view of a person in the crowd.

2 You are cast away on an uninhabited island. What would you hope to find on the island in order to be able to survive?

3 If Lancelot Andrewes had been asked to preach at the Spittle after the defeat of the Armada, what might he have used for the text of his sermon and what might he have said?

4 Describe Christmas in Wales from Belinda Williams' point of view.

5 You have recovered from a long and serious illness. Would you thank God for your return to health and, if so, how would you show your gratitude?

6 Prepare and illustrate a short leaflet for Christian Aid explaining that, since God has been good to us, we should be generous to people less fortunate than ourselves.

7 You have inherited a large sum of money. What charities would you support?

8 Write a hymn suitable for a Harvest Festival.

9 Give some examples from nature of God's generosity.

10 Write a short prayer thanking God for all his gifts.

Things to do

1 Tape-record an interview with Jesus of Nazareth, suitable for use by a broadcasting station.

2 Draw the scene in which the king condemns the crooked treasurer to prison.

3 Design a cover for a book entitled *The Wonders of Nature*.

4 Make a cartoon strip of John Williams' adventures.

5 Find out all you can about London in Lancelot Andrewes' day. Make a plan showing the Pool of London and the site of the Spittle pulpit cross. Suggest a route for the procession.

6 Prepare a school assembly about God's generosity. Use objects from nature, readings from the Bible, poems and songs.

7 Design a poster for 'Friends of the Earth'.

8 Arrange a classroom debate on the motion: 'That we are the most fortunate people in history.'

9 Write and perform a new tune for the hymn 'For the beauty of the earth' (Hymns A & M Revised 171)

10 Design a stained glass window illustrating God's generosity.

1

The lost sheep

Although Jesus' early ministry was centred on Capernaum, he and his disciples wandered from town to town throughout the whole region of Galilee. Sometimes, the little group of men was followed through the countryside by large crowds. All kinds of people wanted to hear Jesus. His stories, in particular, gave people a new and hopeful way of understanding religion. 'He speaks', somebody said, 'like a man with authority, not like the scribes.' Sometimes, too, the scribes came to argue with Jesus.

Most of the scribes were Pharisees, strict religious Jews. Originally, a scribe had been someone who could read and write. Since, before the invention of printing, everything had to be written by hand, a scribe's main task had been the copying of books, especially the books of the Old Testament. But as time went by, the scribes not only copied but edited and interpreted. They became experts in the meaning of the Old Testament. That meant that they were experts in the Torah – the law of Moses given in the first five books of the Bible. The Torah in all its details was complicated in the extreme. There were rules about everything from the treatment of skin disease to the preparation of animals for sacrifice. The Pharisees believed that the Torah was God's finest gift to the Jewish people. It showed that Israel was God's

chosen nation. No other nation in the world mattered. The Torah was God's special favour to his chosen ones and the possession of the law was proof that Israel was separate and holy. The Pharisees, then, were extreme Jewish nationalists who refused to have anything to do with foreigners. And they believed that if Israel kept the Torah in all its details, the Messiah would come to destroy the enemies of Israel. There would then be a golden age when nothing could go wrong for the chosen people.

The teachings of the Pharisees not only separated them from foreigners but also from most ordinary Jews. It was so easy to break the Pharisaic version of the law. It was a crime against God, for instance, to pluck a few ears of corn or to carry a stretcher on the Sabbath day. And, of course, failure to observe some detail or other of the Torah made one a sinner. The Pharisees divided Jewish society into two parts – the sinners and the righteous. No Pharisee would enter the house of a sinner or share a meal at the same table. The chosen ones of Israel should not be contaminated by such company.

The scribes and the Pharisees were scandalized at the behaviour of Jesus of Nazareth. One day, as he was walking along a country road followed by a large crowd, a Pharisee pointed Jesus out to his friends. 'That's the man', he said sneeringly, 'who enters the houses of sinners and eats with them. Any riff-raff is good enough for him!' Jesus stopped and looked around. It was a beautiful day in early summer. The hills, which a few weeks earlier had been green with succulent grass, were now going brown and parched in the hot sun. He could see in the distance a shepherd leading his flock of sheep, picking out the places were there was still pasture. Israelite shepherds always led their sheep in this way. 'Our religion', said Jesus, 'has often described God as the shepherd of Israel. Now a shepherd, like that one over there, was once leading his flock through the parched mountains. At a certain point in the day, he followed his usual custom and counted his sheep. There was one missing. There had been a hundred but now there were ninety-

Modern Jews using the Torah

nine. So he left his flock to fend for itself and retraced his steps, looking for his lost sheep. It was a risky thing to do. There was a real danger that his whole flock would be attacked and killed by wild animals in his absence. But the shepherd felt that the risk was worth taking. He was not prepared to sacrifice even one animal.

'For many miles, the shepherd went unrewarded. It was as though his sheep had disappeared without trace. Then, just as he was about to give up the search, he heard a bleating in the distance. He hurried in the direction of the sound. He found the animal caught in brambles, unable to move. So he took out his knife, cut away the brambles, picked up the sheep and put it around his shoulders. He returned to his flock rejoicing. And when, in the evening, he arrived home in the village, he called his friends and neighbours together and told them the story. And the whole village joined in the party, celebrating the recovery of a lost sheep.'

Then Jesus looked the Pharisee in the eye. 'Sinners', said Jesus, 'are like lost sheep. They are caught in the brambles of their sins. But the great shepherd of Israel will not sacrifice a single one of them. God's heart rejoices with the return of every sinner.'

In this way, Jesus overturned the teachings of the Pharisees. They believed that the most important gift that God had given Israel was the law. But Jesus, instead, taught God's love. God loves and cares for every human being and rejoices when sinners turn to him. God loves, not just Jews but all people. There are no limits to God's love.

Understand your work

1 Describe the beliefs of the Pharisees.

2 Why did the shepherd have a party with his friends and neighbours?

3 What differences were there between the teachings of Jesus and the teachings of the Pharisees?

19

2

Ruth

In the very early days, when judges ruled over Israel, there was once a serious harvest failure in the countryside around Bethlehem. A great deal of the grain rotted during a wet spring and what grew was attacked by a white fungus. Most of the farmers had enough money earned from the good crops of previous years. They bought supplies from other parts of the country. But there was one smallholder called Elimelech for whom the bad harvest was a disaster. He had so little land that one crop failure put him out of business. In a good year, he could only just grow enough to keep his family and his cattle. Now, the winter months lay ahead and his barn was empty. Something had to be done if they were not to starve. So Elimelech sold his cattle, left his land and his house and used what money he had to rent a small cottage in the neighbouring country of Moab. He and his wife, Naomi, spent a bleak winter there with their grown-up but sickly sons, Mahlon and Chilion.

The following year was eventful in the extreme. First, both sons married Moabite women. Mahlon married Orpah and Chilion married Ruth. Then, a few months later, Elimelech died of a heart attack. A short time afterwards, the two brothers died within a week of each other. They were both suffering from tuberculosis. So the three women found themselves alone. 'I must return to Bethlehem,' said Naomi to her daughters-in-law when the period of mourning was over. 'It is right that I should return to the family home. But you stay here in Moab. You are both young enough to marry again.'

Orpah agreed with her mother-in-law and she went back to her parents. But Ruth felt a great concern for Naomi. She knew how hard it would be for a woman living alone. In the short time that she had been part of the family, she had come to love her mother-in-law. 'Do not ask me to leave you and do not forbid me to follow you,' said Ruth. 'Where you go, I will go and where you stay, I will stay. Your people shall be my people and your God will be my God.' Naomi was greatly touched by Ruth's expression of love. The two women left Moab and made their journey to Bethlehem. When they arrived, everyone in the town was saddened by the news of the deaths of Elimelech, Mahlon and Chilion. Naomi returned to the family home and she and Ruth tried to eke out a poverty-stricken existence. Soon after their arrival, it was harvest time again and Ruth joined other poor women as they gleaned after the reapers in the fields.

One of Elimelech's cousins was a wealthy Bethlehem farmer called Boaz. When Boaz saw Ruth, he asked who she was. 'The Moabite woman who looks after your cousin's widow,' came the reply. So Boaz spoke to Ruth. He told her that he had instructed his labourers to treat her with respect and that, if she was hungry or thirsty, she should help herself to the provisions laid on for the harvesters. 'Why are you so kind to me?' asked Ruth. 'Don't you know that I am a foreigner in this land?' 'Everything you have done for your mother-in-law has greatly impressed me,' said Boaz. 'I am only too glad to help you in return.' All the time she was gleaning, Boaz supplied Ruth with food and drink and he instructed his harvesters to leave some of the sheaves of barley for her to collect.

When the harvest had been gathered in, Boaz and his men began the work of threshing. The sheaves of barley were taken to a stone circle on a high piece of ground. All the sheaves were placed in the circle and a yoke of oxen pulled a small threshing machine round and round. The machine had wheels and discs which cut up the straw and shook the grain loose. Then, in the evening when the wind was up, Boaz and his men threw the straw as high as they could into the air. The wind caught the straw and blew it away, leaving the grain to fall to the ground in the stone circle. Threshing was a time of great celebration and the farm women brought prodigious quantities of food and wine for the workers.

That night, tired and full of wine, Boaz went to sleep on a pile of grain. He was startled to be woken at midnight by a young woman who lay at his feet. 'Who are you?' he whispered. 'Ruth,' came the reply. 'I have come to ask a favour of Boaz. I wish to marry.' 'The only man who has a right to

Nicholas Poussin: L'Eté (1660–64). It shows Ruth and Boaz in the harvest field

marry you', said Boaz, 'is Elimelech's nephew. A dead man's next of kin has first right to marry the widow and he is next of kin to Chilion.' So the following day, Boaz requested an audience with ten of the leading citizens of Bethlehem. He and the nephew appeared before them. 'Since you are next of kin,' said Boaz, 'I wish to know your intentions. Naomi has decided to sell the smallholding. Do you wish to buy it?' 'Yes,' replied the nephew. 'Then you must marry Ruth, the Moabite woman,' said Boaz, 'for it is her inheritance you are buying.' At that, the nephew changed his mind. But Boaz turned to the leading citizens. 'You are my witnesses', he said, 'that the nephew has renounced his rights in this matter. I will therefore buy Naomi's property and I will marry Ruth.'

This ancient biblical love story, then, has a happy ending. It is, however, like Jesus' story of the lost sheep, an attack on narrow Jewish nationalism of the type shown by the Pharisees. The story is about a heroine who was not Jewish. But she had become part of God's chosen people because of her love for Naomi and Boaz. 'Your people', Ruth had said, 'shall be my people and your God will be my God.' Like the story of the lost sheep, the book of Ruth is about a God of love. And, at the end of the book, Ruth's importance is driven home by a description of her descendants. Ruth and Boaz had a son called Obed. Obed, in turn, had a son called Jesse. And Jesse was father to David, the greatest of all the kings of Israel. King David himself had a Moabite great-grandmother.

Understand your work

1 Why did Elimelech and his family move to Moab?

2 What trick did Boaz play in order to be able to marry Ruth?

3 Why can the book of Ruth be described as an attack on Pharisaism?

3

The Flood

Old Pete lived in a tatty wooden bungalow standing high on stilts above the level of the roadway. It had been built like that because, years ago, the sea regularly flooded the whole place. Now there was a sea wall and it didn't happen any more. But older properties like this reminded people of what it had been like. In the old days, there had been very few inhabitants of the village. The country road on which it was situated had wandered through the fields to the river estuary where there had been a ferry boat to take people to the shops in the town on the other side. Pete often longed for the old days. He remembered M. Jourbet, the village schoolmaster who was French, and old Canon Aurelius at the Rectory who had a mania for collecting birds' eggs. Now things were different. They had built a bridge over the river and a great main road flashed through the middle of the village, cutting the place in half. The fields, where wheat and barley had once grown, were now entirely inhabited by hundreds and hundreds of caravans. Dairies had been converted into bingo arcades and farmhouses into holiday clubs with fancy names – Pink Flamingo, Kentucky Home and O.K. Saloon. And lots of retired people from the big towns had had bungalows built. Pete had not done badly out of the change. He had a row of petrol pumps outside the bungalow and, in the summer, he sold

petrol from seven in the morning till eleven at night. Pete had a fair bit tucked away in the bank. And he didn't believe in spending it if he could help it. But he couldn't bring himself to like the changes that had taken place in the village. And he didn't much like the people who had come in as a result of the change.

One morning in late September, he woke up to hear water sloshing about under the bungalow. He lay there for a while wondering if he was dreaming. He glanced at his watch. Half-past six. It was just about light. He clambered out of bed and looked out of the window. Disbelief! It was just like the old days. The whole area had become part of the sea. It was a grey, blustery day. The wind seemed to bang against the window from time to time. A caravan was sailing past, like a mini Noah's Ark. Seagulls were scavenging in some floating dustbins. Pete tried to switch on the light and discovered that the electricity was off. He couldn't make tea. So he pulled trousers and an old sweater over his pyjamas, put on waders and an old anorak, then pushed open the front door. The night before, his dinghy had been lying face down in front of the bungalow. Now it was floating face down, its bow jammed between two petrol pumps. It took him half an hour of concerted effort to get the boat, turn it over, fix the outboard, climb in and start the engine.

Pete felt like a gondolier as he buzzed down what had been the main road. The water had transformed the place. The modern houses were a mess, water lapping inside as well as outside ground floor windows. Great branches of trees were floating here and there. Then he caught sight of a face in the window of a bungalow. He steered over and cut his motor as he passed through the gateway. Through the glass, he could see that the old woman's face was grey with shock. 'Come on love,' shouted Pete. She took no notice. 'Open your front door!' he shouted, banging the window for emphasis. 'I'll get you out of there.' She didn't seem able to move. She just stood inside the room, a patchwork shawl clutched round her shoulders, the water lapping round her waist. Pete coaxed and

begged but nothing happened. So he broke the window, opened it, moored the dinghy to the handle and lowered himself into the icy waters of the room. He picked up the old woman and waded to the front door. . . .

The police station was on higher ground, the other side of the village. As Pete beached the dinghy about twenty yards down the road, a couple of ambulance men appeared. They put the old woman on a stretcher and took her away. The place was a hive of activity. There was a helicopter in the field at the back of the police station and a large mobile police unit in the yard at the front. A squad of soldiers was being ordered about by a young officer. A local councillor, amazingly dressed in a smart lounge suit and highly polished shoes, noticed and recognized Pete. Immediately, he was drawn into the official rescue operations. The sea wall had been breached in two places and people had to be rescued from their homes, at least until temporary repairs had been carried out. Pete was joined by a young man in a wet-suit. The pair worked the dinghy from house to house, bringing people to food and warmth at the village school.

When Pete thought about that day later, he was left with a jumble of impressions. There was the old lady who thought that the man in the wet-suit was a Martian who had come to invade her.

There was the housewife who had insisted on going back to her house to rescue the goldfish – in case it drowned! Other memories were not so funny. Homes had been ruined and businesses bankrupted by the coming of the sea. Pete was amazed to discover how few people were insured. In the days that followed, the memories haunted him. In due course, he gave £1,000 of his own money for the Flood Relief fund. It showed the strength of his feelings.

Pete had not liked the coming of the main road, the holiday camps, the caravans and the new people. His heart was still in the village as it had been in the old days. The people of the old days had been prepared for the coming of the sea; expected it even. But when modern defences broke down and the sea came, Pete's heart went out to the new people. They were so vulnerable, so defenceless.

Understand your work

1 What had Pete's village been like in the old days?

2 What was the effect of the flood on the village and its inhabitants?

3 In what ways did Pete's feelings change as a result of the flood?

4

The many faces of love

Now thank we all our God,
  With heart, and hands, and voices,
Who wondrous things hath done,
  In whom his world rejoices;
Who from our mother's arms
  Hath blessed us on our way
With countless gifts of love,
  And still is ours today.
. . . .

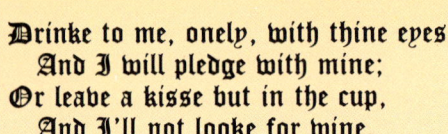

Drinke to me, onely, with thine eyes,
  And I will pledge with mine;
Or leabe a kisse but in the cup,
  And I'll not looke for wine.
. . . .

MICHELLE LOOKED AT THE GLOOMY SCENE, MESMERISED BY THE RAIN. WHY HADN'T GLENN PHONED?

THEN SHE SAW HIM!

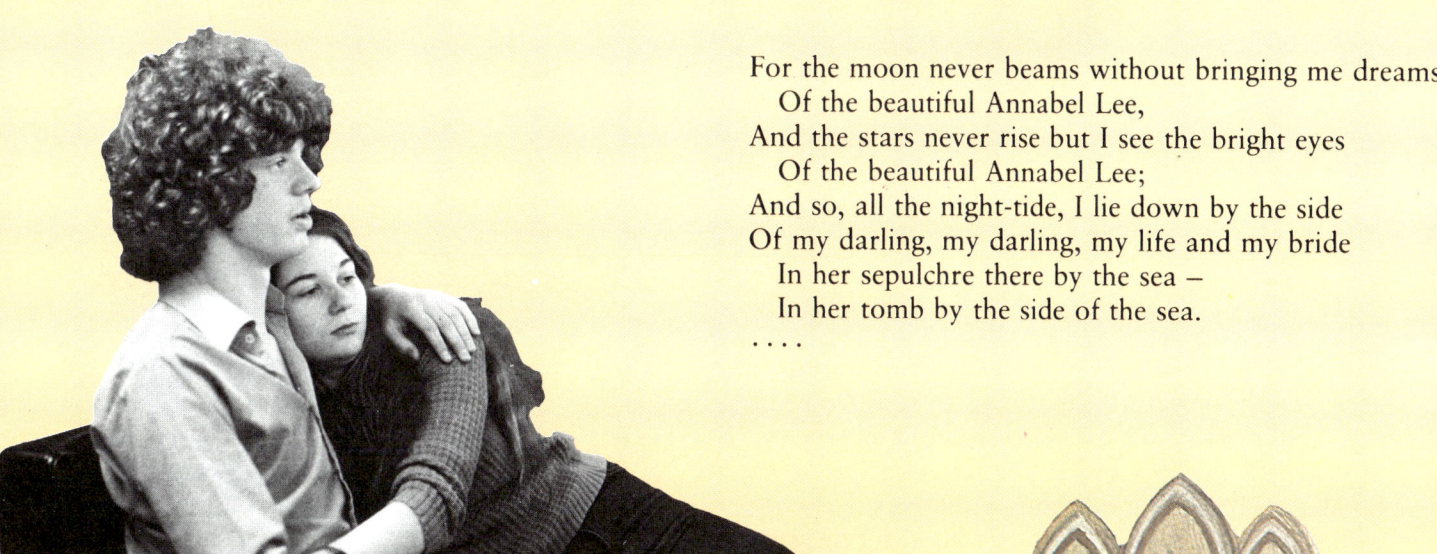

For the moon never beams without bringing me dreams
   Of the beautiful Annabel Lee,
And the stars never rise but I see the bright eyes
   Of the beautiful Annabel Lee;
And so, all the night-tide, I lie down by the side
Of my darling, my darling, my life and my bride
   In her sepulchre there by the sea –
   In her tomb by the side of the sea.
. . . .

Love Divine, all loves excelling,
   Joy of heaven, to earth come down,
Fix in us thy humble dwelling,
   All thy faithful mercies crown.
Jesu, thou art all compassion,
   Pure unbounded love thou art;
Visit us with thy salvation,
Enter every trembling heart.
. . . .

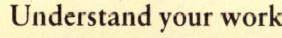

Understand your work

1 Describe Michelle's feelings about Glenn. What other
quotations and illustrations express the same sorts of
feelings?

2 Which of the illustrations and quotations are about
compassionate love?

3 In what ways has the experience of the love of God been
expressed in the pictures and the words?

5

John Donne

Elizabeth I,
by M. Gheeraerts the Younger, 1592 (detail)

There are many kinds of love. In his parable, Jesus compared God with a loving shepherd who went to great lengths in order to recover a stray sheep. The story describes God's compassion for human beings in trouble. The story of Pete's adventures during the flood gives a modern example of the same kind of compassionate love. We are not told that Pete was in any way religious but, at that time, he showed the very qualities which Jesus admired. Such a love can be seen, too, in Ruth's treatment of Naomi. Ruth knew how difficult it would be for Naomi, penniless as she was, to survive in Bethlehem. Ruth's promise, 'Where you go, I will go and where you stay, I will stay', was a remarkable expression of compassionate love.

But there are other kinds of love. There is, for instance, the love between men and women. Christians believe that sexual love is part of God's creation. It was a natural instinct for Michelle to yearn romantically for Glenn and for her to be horrified when she saw him protecting another girl from the rain. Some people make a business out of the natural human desire for such a love. Marriage agencies and dating firms of all kinds, for instance, get lonely people to pay in order to meet other lonely people. There are many ways in which these relationships can go wrong but, when things go well, love between the sexes is one of life's most

rewarding experiences. The story of Ruth, for instance, is not only about her compassionate love for Naomi but also about her marriage to Boaz and the happiness it gave her.

In the course of a lifetime, it is possible for human beings to experience love in a great variety of ways. The life of John Donne provides a good example. He was brought up in London during the reign of Queen Elizabeth I. It was an exciting time in which to live. The court was the most powerful and splendid in the whole of English history. They called the Queen 'Gloriana' and she had command over adventurers like Raleigh and Drake. This, too, was the age of poetry and of the theatre. Shakespeare, the greatest poet and playwright of them all, wrote and acted for a company of players in the city. The main competitors to the theatres were the churches. Plays and sermons were the two main sources of public entertainment. When John Chamberlain wrote to his friend Sir Dudley Carleton about Christmas at court, he explained that 'two excellent sermons were made that day by the Bishop of Winchester and the Bishop of Ely, and a third that afternoon in Paul's, by the Bishop of London, and I heard the Bishop of Rochester as much commended at his parish St. Giles without Cripplegate'. He had attended three sermons on Christmas Day and was sorry to have missed a fourth!

John Donne was born in 1572 and was a young man about town in the early 1590s. Like many others, he attended the Inns of Court where lawyers were trained. He had no intention of being a lawyer. It was simply part of his education. Young Elizabethan men were great collectors of knowledge of all kinds. During this period, Donne wrote a series of brilliant poems. They were passed from hand to hand in manuscript form and much

admired. But they were not to be published during Donne's lifetime. If they had been, it would certainly have caused a scandal. His poems were witty observations on his many love affairs.

In the years that followed, Donne had an eventful but not very successful career. He accompanied the Earl of Essex and Sir Walter Raleigh on an expedition to Cadiz in 1596 and to the Azores in 1597. He became private secretary to the Lord Privy Seal, Sir Thomas Egerton, in 1598. He lost the job four years later when his master found out about his secret marriage to Ann More; a member of Egerton's own family. For the next few years, Donne lived in poverty, unable to get regular work of any kind.

John Donne had been brought up a Roman Catholic but while he was at the Inns of Court, he decided that he preferred to be called simply a Christian. Then, during the poverty-stricken years, a great change came over him. He began to seek and to experience the most remarkable love of which human beings are capable. It is expressed in the great religious poems which he wrote at that time:

> Batter my heart, three person'd God; for you
> As yet but knocke, breathe, shine, and seek to mend;
> That I may rise, and stand, o'erthrow mee,
> 'and bend
> Your force, to breake, blowe, burn and make me new.
> I, like an usurpt towne, to'another due,
> Labour to'admit you . . .

Just as the lovers had longed for each other in his earlier poems, so now Donne longed for God. In this poem, he asks God to attack his heart and complains that God has been too gentle with him. As yet, God had done no more than 'knocke, breathe, shine, and seek to mend' Donne's heart. Instead, Donne reckoned that God should 'breake, blowe, burn and make me new'. God was to 'breake' instead of to 'knocke', to 'blowe' instead of to 'breathe', to 'burn' instead of to 'shine'. Donne's heart should not be mended. It should be made new.

John Donne's intense, personal experience of the love of God led to his becoming a clergyman of the Church of England in 1615. He had experienced sexual love. He had experienced the intense spiritual love of God. Now he was to be a shepherd of God's people, showing compassionate love. In 1621, he became Dean of St. Paul's Cathedral. Donne became a great preacher as well as a great poet.

Understand your work

1 Describe the kinds of love shown in the following examples:
   a The parable of the lost sheep;
   b The cartoon strip about Michelle and Glenn;
   c John Donne's religious poems.

2 During which parts of his life was John Donne concerned with love between the sexes, the love of God and compassionate love?

3 Why did Donne want God to 'breake, blowe, burn and make me new'?

Work Section

Understand your work

1 Why were the Pharisees scandalized when Jesus mixed with all kinds of people?

2 Describe the shepherd's journey in search of his lost sheep.

3 Why did Ruth decide to accompany Naomi to Bethlehem?

4 What kindnesses did Boaz show to Ruth while she was gleaning?

5 How did Pete earn a living?

6 How did Pete rescue the old woman?

7 How do nuns making toys show God's love?

8 What connection do you see between the pictures and the first stanza of the hymn, 'Now thank we all our God'?

9 How can people make money out of the natural human desire for love?

10 What change took place to the character of John Donne during his poverty-stricken years?

Find out more

1 At the end of his conversation with Nicodemus, Jesus explained why God had sent him into the world. Read John 3, 16–18 and answer the following questions:
   a Why did God concern himself with the world?
   b What was God's purpose in sending Jesus into the world?
   c In what way would Christians benefit from their contact with Jesus?

2 Read Leviticus 19, 18. How were the Jews to behave towards each other.

3 The Bible discusses sexual as well as divine love. The Song of Solomon is a collection of love songs. Read The Song of Solomon 1, 5–7 and answer the following questions:
   a How does the lover describe himself?
   b What does he say his brothers made him do?
   c Why has he neglected his own vineyard?
   d What does he want to know about the woman he loves?

4 In the prophecy of Isaiah there is a vision of a world ruled by love. Read Isaiah 11, 6–9 and answer the following questions:
   a Why is it surprising that a wolf shall dwell with a lamb?
   b What other surprising examples does he give?
   c What does the little child do which would normally be very dangerous?
   d What rule does Isaiah lay down for the world of his vision?
   e How could such a thing come about?

5 St. Paul was the first great theologian of the Church. He interpreted Jesus' teachings in a great many different ways. But at the heart of his teachings was the idea of Christian love. Read 1 Corinthians 13, 1–13 and answer the following questions:
   a What does St. Paul say he is like if he lacks love?
   b What qualities are useless without love?
   c What are the qualities of love itself?
   d What does St. Paul say about knowledge and prophecy?
   e Why does he compare himself to a child and what does he hope for in the future?
   f What are the three qualities of Christianity and which is the most important?

6 In about the year 326AD, a young man called Cyril began work as a deacon in the great church called the Martyry, built at the expense of the Emperor Constantine on the site of Golgotha, the place where Jesus was crucified. It was regarded as a particularly holy place where devils would fear to come. Later in his life, St. Cyril became bishop of Jerusalem but, at that time, one of the most important tasks he undertook was the preparation of candidates for baptism. This took place during Lent and the baptism itself took place on the eve of Easter. St. Cyril's lectures have survived. Read the extract and answer the following questions:

   So far, your names have been enrolled and you have been called up for service. The lamps have been kindled for the wedding procession. There is longing for the citizenship of heaven. There is good intention, with hope to back it up. He cannot lie that saith 'All things work together for good to them that love God'.

   a What is the first thing that St. Cyril has done with the candidates for baptism?
   b Read Matthew 25, 1–13. How does St. Cyril refer to this parable?
   c How are faith, hope and love represented in St. Cyril's discussion?

7 There is a little prayer which appears in some prayer books called the Collect. Nobody knows for certain the origin of the word but it probably comes from the Latin phrase 'plebe collecta', which means 'the people being gathered together. Here is the Collect for the Fourteenth Sunday after Trinity taken from the Book of Common Prayer:

   Almighty and everlasting God, give unto us the increase of faith, hope and charity; and, that we may obtain that which thou dost promise, make us to love that which thou dost command; through Jesus Christ our Lord.

Answer the following questions:

a What two qualities does the prayer ascribe to God?

b What qualities does the prayer seek for Christians?

c What help does the prayer ask for Christians in order that they may receive the promises of God?

8 Find out all you can about Mother Teresa. In what ways has her work been an expression of Christian love?

9 Here is a poem called 'Three rusty nails' by Roger McGough:

Mother, there's a strange man
Waiting at the door
With a familiar sort of face
You feel you've seen before.

Says his name is Jesus
Can we spare a couple of bob
Says he's been made redundant
And now can't find a job.

Yes I think he's a foreigner
Egyptian or a Jew
Oh aye and that reminds me
He'd like some water too.

Well shall I give him what he wants
Or send him on his way?
O.K. I'll give him 5p
Say that's all we've got today.

And I'll forget about the water
I suppose it's a bit unfair
But honest, he's filthy dirty
All beard and straggly hair.

       *   *   *

Mother, he asked about the water
I said the tank had burst
Anyway I gave him the coppers
That seemed to quench his thirst,

He said it was little things like that
That kept him on the rails
Then he gave me his autographed picture
And these three rusty nails.

Answer the following questions:

a Who does the child say has come to the door?

b How is the stranger described?

c What does the mother tell the child to do?

d How does the child explain to the stranger that he can't have water?

e Read Matthew 25, 31–40. What connection can you see between this poem and verse 40?

f Of what are we being reminded when the child is given the rusty nails?

10 Here is part of a modern prayer by Michel Quoist:

Lord, why did you tell me to love all men, my
brothers?
I have tried, but I come back to you frightened....

Lord, I was so peaceful at home, I was so
comfortably settled.
I was well furnished and I felt cosy.
I was alone, I was at peace,
Sheltered from the wind, the rain, the mud.
I would have stayed unsullied in my ivory tower.
But, Lord, you have discovered a breach in my
defences,
You have forced me to open my door,
Like a squall of rain in the face, the cry of men has
awakened me ... and, rashly enough, I left my
door ajar. Now, Lord, I am lost!
Outside men were lying in wait for me
I did not know they were so near; in this house, in
this street, in this office; my neighbour, my
colleague, my friend.
As soon as I started to open the door I saw them,
with outstretched hands, burning eyes, longing
hearts, like beggars on church steps.

Answer the following questions:

a What did Quoist want to do if left to himself?

b What happened when he felt forced to try to love other people?

c Why does he describe himself as lost?

d How does he describe all the people who are longing to be loved?

e Why are they like 'beggars on church steps'?

Use your imagination

1 Tell the story of the 'Lost Sheep' from the shepherd's point of view.

2 Write a letter from Boaz to a friend explaining that he is about to marry Ruth.

3 Describe Pete's life as a child in the village.

4 Continue the cartoon about Michelle and Glenn.

5 Describe the scene when Sir Thomas Egerton found out about John Donne's secret marriage to Ann More.

6 Write a short prayer about Christian love.

7 Here is the beginning of a short story:

The great surging crowd stood below the balcony on
which the preacher was standing. He was not only a
clergyman but also the leader of a great national
movement. 'All men, regardless of their colour,
should have equal rights,' he said. 'The day will come
when this will be so.' Suddenly a bullet whistled
through the air and smacked into the wall behind
him. An attempted assassination! ...

Now continue.

8 Write a poem about a tramp visiting your house.

9 Your friend is getting married. Write a letter of congratulation.

10 The father of one of the boys at your school has been sent to prison after being charged with theft. How do you treat the boy?

The parables of the kingdom

Just north of Capernaum, the edge of the Sea of Galilee formed a series of semi-circular creeks which looked for all the world like a number of amphitheatres. In the springtime, when the snows on Mount Hermon had melted, the water-level in the lake rose considerably and it was possible to sail right into one of these creeks. On one occasion, when a large crowd wanted to listen to him, Jesus took advantage of this. He sat in the bow of a fishing boat belonging to his disciple, Simon Peter, and talked to the people sitting on the sloping shore.

As usual, Jesus' teaching took the form of story-telling. The stories, or parables as they are called, were usually based on events and people in the Galilee of Jesus' day. If a man had fallen into debt or a sheep had gone astray, it provided Jesus with an idea for a story. There was, for instance, a local merchant who had made a complete fool of himself. He had sold his house and everything he had in order to buy one immensely valuable pearl. Now he had scarcely enough to eat and did nothing but gloat stupidly over his new possession. The people in the market laughed at him and were sorry for his wife and children. Jesus had only to mention his name for people to burst out laughing at what the silly man had done. 'What a lunatic!' said Jesus.

'But he has a great lesson to teach us.' His audience immediately stopped laughing and waited to hear what Jesus would say. 'We need', said Jesus, 'to be as single-minded about the kingdom of heaven as the merchant is about his pearl.'

'Think', said Jesus, 'about that man who found a bag of money in a field not far from here. He too sold all his possessions and he borrowed money in order to buy the field. But it paid handsome dividends.' The people in Jesus' audience nodded. He was now a successful Capernaum businessman. 'It was a terrible risk,' said Jesus. 'Supposing someone had found out what he was up to. The bag of money might have been taken away before he owned the property.' Jesus paused. Everyone was listening intently. 'But like the businessman,' said Jesus, 'we too have a hidden treasure. It is called the kingdom of heaven and for its sake we too must take risks.'

Then Jesus went on to remind his audience of how a woman makes bread. When the flour has been ground and mixed with water and a little salt, she adds the yeast. Then she kneads the dough and leaves it in the sun. At first, nothing happens. Then, slowly, the yeast makes the dough rise. Soon it is twice the size it was at first. 'The kingdom of heaven', said Jesus, 'is like the yeast in the dough. It

A woman making bread   The merchant with the pearl

ferments imperceptibly at first. But just as the yeast changes the dough, so the kingdom will entirely change a person's character.' Then Jesus pointed at a field in the distance. There was a farmer walking across the grass sowing seed everywhere. He had a bag of corn slung over his left shoulder and he plunged his right hand into the bag and swept handfuls of seed onto the ground. Farmers in Jesus' day sowed first, then ploughed the ground. 'Look how careless he is,' said Jesus. 'The corn falls everywhere. It falls on the pathway, in the rocky soil and on the brambles. But the farmer isn't worried. He knows that enough seed will fall into good soil for him to receive an excellent harvest.' Jesus looked around and smiled at the intent faces of his listeners. 'And God isn't worried either,' said Jesus. 'He will have a great harvest of believers just as the farmer will fill his granary with corn.'

As he told his stories, people began to understand what Jesus meant by the kingdom of heaven. He was not talking about a place but about a way of life. A member of the kingdom belongs to a society which values God in the same way as the stupid merchant valued his pearl. Such people think of God as a treasure for whom they will take any risk. And God comes into their lives as yeast comes into the dough. At first nothing seems to happen

The sower

but in the end a person's whole life is changed.

Jesus told a great many parables that day. His teachings were full of hope for all those ordinary people who came to listen to him. The leaders of the synagogues would have described most of them as sinners and would have had nothing to do with them. But Jesus taught that God spreads his kingdom with the same carelessness as a first-century Palestinian farmer sowed his seed. And just as the seed fell everywhere but turned into a great harvest, so God's kingdom is spread everywhere and all kinds of people will respond. As might be expected when Jesus was sitting in the bow of a fishing vessel on the Sea of Galilee, one of his parables was about fishing. 'The kingdom of heaven', said Jesus, 'is like a net which was thrown into the sea and gathered in fish of every kind.' That too was a message of hope.

Understand your work

1 How did the story of the merchant enable Jesus to teach his followers about the kingdom of heaven?

2 What was the point of Jesus' story about the woman who made a loaf?

3 What stories did Jesus tell to prove that God did not restrict his kingdom to certain types of people?

The dragnet

The study of the parables

It is not easy to date Jesus' crucifixion but scholars think it took place in AD 33. About fifteen years later, St. Paul wrote his letter to the Galatians, the first of his long series of letters. About thirty years after the crucifixion, St. Mark wrote the first gospel. There were, we know, other writings of which no copies have survived but it is clear that the story of Jesus' life and teachings was conveyed for many years by word of mouth. Fortunately, a great deal of Jesus' teaching took the form of story-telling. He had an ingenious and original mind and the parables were an effective way of conveying his ideas to the ordinary people who came to listen to him. The stories also had the advantage of being easy to remember. Consequently, they supply us with the most reliable examples of Jesus' teaching in the New Testament. During the period when very little had been written, it was easy for parts of Jesus' teaching to be forgotten and other parts to be changed, but the parables, because they were in the form of memorable stories, were less liable to alteration than the rest.

Most of the parables were based on ordinary life in the Galilee of Jesus' day. If a farmer was sowing in his field or fishermen were working their nets, Jesus used such events in order to explain his teachings. The stories were simple but they were never quite straightforward. There was always something to think about long after the story had been told. Jesus had found something to admire in the foolhardiness of a merchant who had sold all his possessions in order to own a single pearl. He was interested in a farmer's carelessness as he scattered his seed everywhere, even on the rocks and in the brambles. Long after the event, people would still be intrigued by the story of the successful businessman who had started by finding a bag of money in a field. Such events helped people to remember Jesus' teachings. Yet, between Jesus' time and the writing of the New Testament, there were certainly changes even when it came to the parables. In those years when people told and re-told the stories, certain alterations took place. It is possible to study those alterations.

One way of doing so is by comparing the

St. Mark

different gospels. In the years when nothing was written down, collections of parables gradually came into existence. Each group of Jesus' followers had, for instance, a different collection of parables about the kingdom of heaven. A comparison of St. Mark's version with St. Matthew's account of the same occasion shows this very clearly. Both gospels begin by saying that Jesus sat in a boat and taught the people on the shore. But the parables about the merchant and his pearl, about the bag of money in a field, about the yeast in the dough and about the fishermen with their drag-net do not appear in St. Mark's version. He has other parables of the kingdom. There is a parable, for instance, about seed growing secretly. It is reminiscent of the parable of the yeast in the dough. At first a field that has been sowed does not change. Then, in due time, the whole character of the field changes with the appearance of the new corn. And St. Mark supplies another of those parables in which Jesus made his audience laugh. 'Supposing', said Jesus, 'somebody was fool enough to put a bushel over a candle.' A bushel was a container for measuring corn. Candles were very expensive. The idea was absurd. Nobody in his senses would up-turn a bushel and put it over a candle. 'But that's exactly what the leaders of the synagogues are doing,' said Jesus. 'They are hiding the light of God's kingdom from the people.' Although St. Mark and St. Matthew, then, were both describing Jesus' teachings from the boat, each had a different collection of parables for the occasion.

The other important change that took place was that people made the stories more complicated than they had been when Jesus told them. Both St. Mark and St. Matthew supply us with an elaborate version of the parable of the sower. Every little detail in the story is given a religious meaning. The sower is Jesus, the preacher. The seeds are his teachings. The various types of soil are the different kinds of people who hear his preaching. Most of them reject his ideas. There are people with minds like rocky soil. They have no depth of character and soon forget what Jesus taught. There are people with minds like soil covered in brambles. Just as the young shoots of corn are choked by the brambles, so Jesus' teachings are choked by the cares and pleasures and riches of this life. There are people with minds like the pathway. They are so unreceptive that the seed never has a chance. In making this story more elaborate, though, both St. Matthew and St. Mark have forgotten the original meaning. They have become much more interested in the seed that is wasted than in the seed that bears fruit. Jesus had predicted that God would have a great harvest of believers just as the farmer would fill his granary with corn. But St. Matthew and St. Mark say that only a few seeds actually bring forth fruit and that most of Jesus' followers will fall by the wayside.

The study of the parables, then, is fascinating because it brings us near to the actual teachings of Jesus of Nazareth. The stories themselves come to

St. Matthew

us virtually unchanged since Jesus used them to explain his religious ideas. But in those years before the stories were written down, the original time and place of a parable were forgotten and people read all kinds of extra meanings into the stories. Sometimes, the process led to conclusions which Jesus had not intended.

Understand your work

1 Why are the parables the most reliable examples of Jesus' teachings in the New Testament?

2 Explain the parables of the seed growing secretly and of the candle under the bushel.

3 What changes took place to the parables between the time when Jesus told the stories and the time when the evangelists wrote them down?

The Victorian way of death

Jesus' parables of the kingdom described a way of life. The people who belonged to the kingdom put God before all else. God was like a priceless pearl, like a hidden treasure or like a seed growing secretly in the soil. God changed a person's whole character. After Jesus, his followers carried on his teachings. But as circumstances changed, so did the understanding of what he taught. St. Mark and St. Matthew, for instance, wrote their gospels for Christians later in the first century. By that time, the Christian Church was well established and growing rapidly. It explains why the parable of the sower was differently understood. Jesus told the story to give hope to the ordinary people who were not welcomed into the synagogues. But St. Mark and St. Matthew wrote the story to encourage people who were members of the Church. So in the gospels, Christians are warned not to be like those people who had minds like rocky soil or soil covered in brambles. Jesus was predicting a great harvest but St. Mark and St. Matthew were warning Christians that they must persevere in order to be like the good corn which brought forth fruit.

And in Christianity, Jesus' teachings have continued to be understood in different ways at different times. Henry Francis Lyte's teachings about the kingdom of heaven, for instance were quite different from those of Jesus. Lyte was Perpetual Curate of Lower Brixham in Devon. He

Henry Francis Lyte

Lower Brixham Church in 1824

died in Nice on 20th November, 1847. He was well-known as a writer of hymns and poems, many of which had been published during his lifetime. Three years after his death, a book of his writings called *Remains* was published with a preface written by his daughter. In it, she describes his last days at Lower Brixham and the composition of his most famous hymn:

The summer was passing away, and the month of September (that month in which he was once more to quit his native land) arrived, and each day seemed to have a special value as being one day nearer his departure. His family was surprised and almost alarmed at his announcing his intention of preaching once more to his people. His weakness, and the

A Victorian funeral

possible danger attending the effort, were urged to prevent it, but in vain. 'It was better', as he used often playfully to say, when in comparative health, 'to wear out than to rust out.' He felt that he should be enabled to fulfil his wish, and feared not the result. His expectation was well founded. He did preach, and amid the breathless attention of his hearers gave them the sermon on the Holy Communion.... He afterwards assisted at the administration of the Holy Eucharist, and though necessarily much exhausted by the exertion and excitement of his effort, yet his friends had no reason to believe it had been hurtful to him. In the evening of the same day he placed in the hands of a near and dear relative the little hymn 'Abide with me', with an air of his own composing adapted to the words.

The tune that Lyte wrote was replaced, a few years later, by one written by W. H. Monk which became immensely popular. It is the tune which is used both in church and at football matches today.

Jesus never gave a precise description of what happened to people after they had died. Jesus' emphasis was on life. Yet in Victorian times, it was firmly believed that death would lead immediately to judgement and to eternal heaven or hell. Lyte's hymn was written in the knowledge that his own death was very near:

Abide with me; fast falls the eventide;
The darkness deepens; Lord with me abide;
When other helpers fail, and comforts flee,
Help of the helpless, O abide with me.

Swift to its close ebbs out life's little day;
Earth's joys grow dim, its glories pass away;
Change and decay in all around I see;
O Thou, Who changest not, abide with me.

I need Thy Presence every passing hour;
What but Thy grace can foil the tempter's power?
Who like Thyself my guide and stay can be?
Through cloud and sunshine, Lord, abide with me.

I fear no foe with Thee at hand to bless;
Ills have no weight, and tears no bitterness;
Where is death's sting? Where, Grave, thy victory?
I triumph still, if Thou abide with me.

Hold Thou Thy Cross before my closing eyes;
Shine through the gloom, and point me to the skies;
Heav'n's morning breaks, and earth's vain shadows flee;
In life, in death, O Lord, abide with me.

The hymn was written on 4th September, 1847. Oddly, it has been placed in *Hymns Ancient and Modern* among the evening hymns.

Understand your work

1 Why did St. Mark and St. Matthew draw a different meaning from the parable of the sower?

2 What happened on the day when Lyte wrote the hymn?

3 How does Lyte give the impression that he believes heaven to be a place beyond space and time?

4

St. Simeon Stylites

Silver reliquary showing St Simeon Stylites

St. Simeon Stylites established his own version of the kingdom of heaven on a mountainous spur in northern Syria in the fifth century. The final arrangements were not quite what Simeon had envisaged when he had gone to that remote, rocky terrain. He had aimed at a simple life of self denial and prayer. He had expected to inhabit a cell in which he could devote his life entirely to God. He was as single-minded as the merchant who had bought the pearl in Jesus' parable. But unfortunately, people heard about this lonely hermit and they flocked in large numbers to visit him. So Simeon decided, quite literally, to rise above his problem. He began to build himself a pillar which would raise him above the level of his admirers. At first the pillar was quite small but as the years went by it grew and grew to a final height of about fourteen metres. His fame spread far and wide and, over the years, people came in their thousands to admire Simeon standing, sitting, kneeling or sleeping on the top of his pillar. It became a great place of pilgrimage and people often went there to pray.

Simeon had been born in AD 390. His father was probably a wealthy farmer. At the age of sixteen, however, Simeon decided that he had no interest in farming and that he wanted to become a monk. He joined a monastery at Telade and stayed there for six years. It was a well organized monastery where the monks not only prayed together but shared all kinds of other activities like horticulture and cooking. Simeon gradually became more and more discontented with monastic routine. His life seemed too well organized, too easy. He believed that total effort should be concentrated on God and that all other activities were a waste of time. Human needs were not important. Only prayer was important.

As time went by, Simeon increasingly did without food and sleep. He forced his body to stand for hours on end. He decided that washing himself and changing his clothes were a waste of time. Slowly, he came to the conclusion that the unwashed state was particularly holy. Soon, maggots began to fall out of his clothing, and his fellow monks asked Simeon to leave because they could stand the smell no more. He joined a smaller monastery at Telnessin. There, he asked the monks to do without food for the forty days of Lent. The monks disagreed and there was a great argument.

The church of St Simeon Stylites as it is today

At last, it was agreed that they would put Simeon in a walled-up cell with ten loaves and a large urn of water. When the monks broke into the cell at the end of Lent, they found Simeon unconscious and the loaves and the water untouched. After about three years at the monastery, Simeon decided to go and live by himself in a cell. That was the cell at which people began to visit him in large numbers and which led him to the decision to build his pillar.

During his time on the top of the pillar, Simeon received a basket of food every day from the ground, except during Lent when he did not eat at all. Visitors were sometimes allowed to climb up a ladder in order to speak to him. He spent a great deal of every day doing exercises. He would, for instance bend and touch his toes as many as two thousand times. It was a way of bowing to God and keeping fit at the same time. Sometimes he preached sermons from his pillar to the crowds who came to see him. The bishops and leaders of the church at the time had a great respect for Simeon. They often sent to him for advice so that, although Simeon never went anywhere, he had a great deal of influence on the way in which the Church was run at the time. Simeon's strange way of life, though, seems to have done him little harm. He lived until he was nearly seventy years old and, after he died in AD 459, his admirers built the largest church in the world at the time at the base of his pillar. A whole town of hostels, inns, monasteries and churches grew around the place where he had built his pillar and the ruin of the great church of St Simeon Stylites is there to this day. It was all done in admiration for a hairy, dirty and peculiar saint who hadn't a single possession in the world apart from a pillar.

When H. F. Lyte wrote the words of 'Abide with me', he was expressing the belief, strong in Victorian times, that death is a gateway to the kingdom of heaven. St. Simeon Stylites' life at the top of a pillar, too, reflected the ideas of his time. The people of the sixth century admired great feats of self-denial and endurance. After Simeon, a great many 'stylites' as they were called built pillars and lived on top of them. In the end a law had to be passed prohibiting such activities.

Understand your work

1 Why did Simeon Stylites become discontented with monastic life?

2 Why did he build his pillar?

3 Why did a large town grow up at the site of Simeon's pillar?

5

Thy kingdom come

From the earliest times, the Jews regarded themselves as God's chosen people. They believed that the day would come, some time in the future, when God would punish all sinners and would destroy all the enemies of Israel. The day of the Lord, as they called it, was associated with the coming of the Messiah, the holy leader whom God would send to rule over them. 'The government will be upon his shoulder,' wrote the prophet Isaiah, 'and his name will be called "Wonderful Counsellor, Mighty God, Everlasting Father, Prince of Peace". Of the increase of his government and of peace there will be no end.' The Jews expected the Messiah to come on the day of the Lord with power and great glory. His coming would begin a reign of peace and prosperity during which Israel would be recognized as the greatest nation on earth.

For the Christians, these ideas were changed by Jesus of Nazareth. During the time that they were with Jesus, the disciples gradually came to the conclusion that he really was the Messiah so long expected by the Jews. Yet there were many differences between the Old Testament descriptions of the Messiah and the realities of Jesus' life. He had not come as a king. He had been born of humble parentage and had been brought up in Nazareth. He did not wield great political power. Indeed, when power was offered to him, he refused it. And far from punishing sinners, he spent most of his time teaching them. There was no sign, furthermore, that he was about to raise an army in order to destroy the Romans, the present enemies of Israel. The day of the Lord, if that is what it was, had turned out quite differently from what had been expected by generations of Jews. Jesus was gentle rather than powerful and humble rather than proud.

Whenever Jesus' disciples questioned him about the day of the Lord, he always said that such things could safely be left to God. 'It is not for you', said Jesus when he was taking leave of his disciples for the last time, 'to know times or seasons which the Father has fixed by his own authority.' Unlike the Jewish religious leaders who expected God's power and glory to come on a day in the future for the benefit of the Jewish nation, Jesus was concerned to show that God can change human life here and now. His teachings were primarily concerned with the present. The kingdom of heaven ferments in the mind like yeast in the dough. It grows like seed developing secretly in the soil. The kingdom can change a person's whole character. It is like a tiny mustard seed which falls into the ground and grows to such a size that the birds of the air make their nests in it. And Jesus was not like the synagogue leaders who hid God's light like a candle under a bushel. He preached the kingdom of heaven to all and sundry. He was like a fisherman hauling all kinds of different fish in a drag-net. Jesus' desire was to convert the whole world to the kingdom of heaven. So he taught his disciples to pray:

> 'Thy kingdom come,
> Thy will be done
>   On earth as it is in heaven.'

The Chapel of the Ascension, Jerusalem

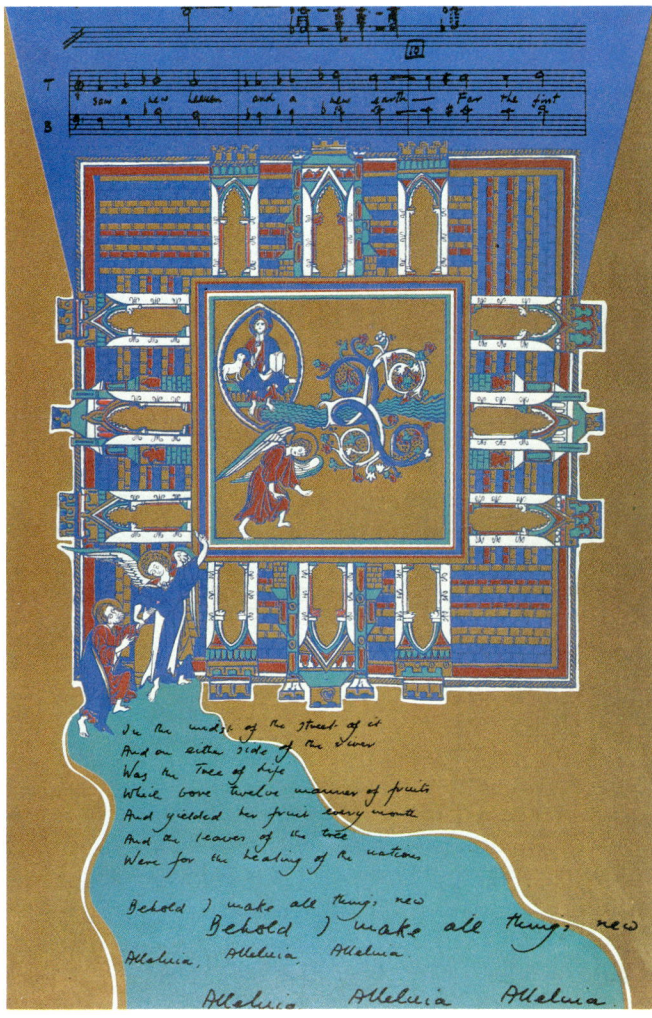

An artist's impression of The New Jerusalem

God's kingdom would come if people did God's will on earth in the present.

The Christians of the early Church had great problems with Jesus' teachings about the kingdom of heaven. The disciples and their followers were nearly all Jews, brought up to believe in the day of the Lord. They quickly came to the conclusion that Jesus would soon return to earth in power and great glory. They believed that the end of the evil world in which they lived was close at hand. As the writer of the Revelation to John, the last book of the New Testament, explains, he had a vision in which he 'saw a new heaven and a new earth; for the first heaven and the first earth had passed away.' So strong was this expectation in the early Church that it explains why there was such a long time between Jesus' life and the writing of the first gospel. There seemed little point in producing written records when the end of all things was at hand. It only gradually dawned on the early Church that Jesus had never promised anything of the sort.

And since the days of the early Church, Jesus' teachings about the kingdom have been interpreted in a great many different ways. Like Jesus, St. Simeon Stylites was concerned with the present. He certainly showed the sort of single-mindedness that Jesus had talked about in his parable of the merchant and the valuable pearl. And certainly, his way of life was greatly affected by his beliefs. But Jesus never told his followers to become hermits or to inflict great sufferings on themselves. In Victorian Christianity, on the other hand, the emphasis was all on God's kingdom in the future. H. F. Lyte expected to experience the kingdom of heaven immediately after his death.

Most modern Christians are much more concerned with seeking God's will for the present rather than looking forward to some time in the future. The main service in many Christian churches is the Holy Communion at which Christians are reminded of the presence of Christ in their midst. When they leave at the end of the service, they feel that they are taking Christ with them into the streets and homes, shops and factories. Few preachers, these days, speak of the end of the world in their sermons – perhaps because, in the age of atomic weapons, such an event is quite possible. But if it were to happen, it would have little to do with the coming of God's kingdom.

Understand your work

1 What was the Old Testament teaching about the day of the Lord?

2 Why did it take such a long time after Jesus' life before the first gospel was written?

3 How do modern Christians understand Jesus' teachings about the kingdom?

Work Section

Understand your work

1 How was Jesus able to compare the kingdom to a woman making bread?

2 What is the parable of the drag-net about?

3 Why are parables found in groups in the New Testament?

4 When the gospel writers made the parable of the sower more complicated, how did this change the meaning of the story?

5 What differences are there between Jesus' teaching about the kingdom of heaven and the ideas found in the hymn 'Abide with me'?

6 Why is it odd that, in *Hymns Ancient and Modern*, the humn 'Abide with me' is put among the evening hymns? How could such a mistake have come about?

7 Write a short account of the life of St. Simeon Stylites.

8 What influence did Simeon have on the church of the time?

9 How do the parables of the kingdom show that Jesus was much more interested in the present than in the future?

10 How did social conditions in Victorian England affect the idea of the kingdom of heaven and why do modern preachers rarely discuss the end of the world?

Find out more

1 Read Luke 5, 1–11 and answer the following questions:

  a What does Luke tell us of Jesus' teaching from the boat?

  b Why did Simon at first refuse to go fishing?

  c Why did Simon call another boat?

  d What did Jesus mean when he said that henceforth Simon would be catching men?

  e What happened to the fishing net?

  f How do these events remind one of the parables of the pearl and of the money hidden in the field?

2 In St. Luke's Gospel, the kingdom is compared to a great banquet. Read Luke 14, 15–24 and answer the following questions:

  a Who gave the banquet?

  b What excuses were made by the various guests?

  c What did the host do about it?

3 The story of the great banquet also appears in St. Matthew's Gospel but it has been made much more complicated. Read Matthew 22, 1–11 and answer the following questions:

  a Who gave the banquet?

  b Why was it given?

  c How does it remind us that Jesus was described as the 'son of God'?

  d If Jesus is the son, who is the father?

  e In St. Luke's Gospel, the banquet is Jesus' teachings but what does the marriage feast represent in St. Matthew's version?

  f In St. Luke's Gospel there is only one servant, but St. Matthew describes many. Who do they represent?

  g How did the invited guests treat the servants?

  h What connection does this have with the way in which the Christians of the early Church were treated by the Jews?

  i How does St. Matthew hint at the defeat of the Jews by the Romans and the destruction of the Temple in AD 70?

  j How does this help us to date St. Matthew's Gospel?

4 As with the parable of the sower, when the gospel writer makes the story more complicated he also changes its meaning. In St. Matthew's Gospel, the story of the banquet also gets into a muddle at the end. If the wedding feast represents the kingdom of heaven, there are both bad and good people there. St. Matthew tried to correct this by adding a second parable. Read Matthew 22, 11–14 and answer the following questions:

  a How does Matthew show that evil people will be thrown out of the kingdom of heaven?

  b How is this parable reminiscent of Jesus' story of the weeds in the cornfield in Matthew 13, 24–30?

5 Isaac Watts (1674–1748) was a minister of the Independent church and the writer of many fine English hymns. Like St. Matthew, he was fond of making elaborate comparisons. Read Deuteronomy 34, 1–6 and compare it with his hymn:

There is a land of pure delight,
  Where saints immortal reign;
Infinite day excludes the night,
  And pleasures banish pain.

There everlasting spring abides,
  And never-withering flowers;
Death, like a narrow stream, divides
  This heavenly land from ours

Sweet fields beyond the swelling flood
  Stand dressed in living green;
So to the Jew old Canaan stood,
  While Jordan rolled between.

But timorous mortals start and shrink
  To cross this narrow sea,
And linger shivering on the brink,
  And fear to launch away.

O could we make our doubts remove,
  Those gloomy doubts that rise,

And see the Canaan that we love
  With unbeclouded eyes!

Could we but climb where Moses stood,
  And view the landscape o'er,
Not Jordan's stream, nor death's cold flood
  Should fright us from the shore!

Answer the following questions:
a With what does Watts compare the Jordan?
b What, in Watts' hymn, is the equivalent of the land of Canaan?
c Who died before the Israelites arrived in the promised land?
d How does Watts' hymn describe the fear of death?
e In what ways is this hymn similar to 'Abide with me'?

6 But the idea of God and the way in which he is described changes continually. Here are some quotations from Exodus, St. John's Gospel, Chaucer's *Canterbury Tales*, a Victorian hymn by A. Midlane and a modern hymn by Sidney Carter. But which is which?

a *There's a Friend for little children*
  Above the bright blue sky,
  A Friend who never changes,
  Whose love will never die . . .

b *. . . for I the Lord your God am a jealous God, visiting the iniquity of the fathers upon the children to the third and fourth generation of those that hate me and showing steadfast love to thousands of those who love me and keep my commandments.*

c *. . . that thanke I oure lord Jesus Christ and his blisful moder, and alle the seintes of hevene; bisekinge hem that they hennesforth, un-to my lyves ende, send me grace to biwayle my giltes, and studie the salvacioun of my soule . . .*

d *When I needed a neighbour, were you there,*
  were you there?
  When I needed a neighbour, were you there?
  And the creed and the colour and the name won't matter,
  Were you there?

e *For God so loved the world that he gave his only Son, that whoever believes in him should not perish but have eternal life.*

7 Revelation 21, 1–7 is a passage from the Bible often read at funerals. Study the passage and answer the following questions:
a How does the writer remind us of St. Matthew's version of the parable of the great banquet?
b Why are Alpha and Omega mentioned?
c Is the emphasis of the passage on life or on death?
d In what ways might this passage comfort people at a funeral?

8 The teachings of modern theologians, trying to get rid of the idea of a God 'out beyond the world', have been too complicated for most ordinary people to understand. Here is a quotation from 'Mister God this is Anna' by Fynn, published in 1974:

'The diffrense from a person and an angel is easy. Most of an angel is in the inside and most of a person is on the outside.' These are the words of six-year old Anna, sometimes called Mouse, Hum or Joy. At five years Anna knew absolutely the purpose of being, knew the meaning of love and was a personal friend and helper of Mister God. At six, Anna was a theologian, mathematician, philosopher, poet and gardener. If you asked her a question you would get an answer – in due course. On some occasions, the answer would be delayed for weeks or months; but eventually, in her own good time, the answer would come: direct, simple and much to the point.
   She never made eight years, she died by an accident. She died with a grin on her beautiful face. She died saying, 'I bet God lets me into heaven for this', and I bet he did too.

Answer the following questions:
a What did Anna mean by the difference between a person and an angel?
b How did Anna develop between the ages of five and six?
c Read Mark 10, 15. How was Anna an example of Jesus' teaching?
d What was Anna's idea of heaven?

9 Fynn, like Jesus, admired a child-like faith. But the ideas which attracted one generation can have the opposite effect on us. The people of the fifth century flocked to admire St. Simeon Stylites on his pillar but the modern poet, A. G. Prys-Jones, had rather different ideas about the life of a hermit:

St. Govan

St. Govan, he built him a cell
By the side of the Pembroke sea,
And there, as the crannied seagulls dwell,
In a tiny, secret citadel
He sighed for eternity.

St. Govan, he built him a cell
Between the wild sky and the sea,
Where the sunsets redden the rolling swell
And brooding splendour has thrown her spell
On valley and moorland lea.

St. Govan still lies in his cell
But his soul, long since, is free
And one may wonder – and who can tell –
If good St. Govan likes Heaven as well
As his cell by the sounding sea?

Answer the following questions:
a Describe the position of St. Govan's cell.
b In what way was his position similar to that of St. Simeon Stylites?
c What was St. Govan's ambition?
d How does the poet show his doubts about St. Govan's ideas?

10 Copy some inscriptions from the tombstones in a local churchyard or cemetery. What do they tell you about the ideas of the people who placed them there?

A woman caught in adultery

'You must learn to recognize the signs of the times,' said Jesus. He pointed at a fig tree which was growing at the entrance to one of the houses in the little square where he and his audience were standing. 'All winter', said Jesus, 'that tree stood there gaunt and straggly. People did not know whether it was dead or alive. The bare branches rattled in the wind. But look at the tree now!' The little tree was shimmering in the spring sunshine, its branches covered in tiny green leaves and young fruit. 'The kingdom of heaven', said Jesus, 'is like a fig tree in the spring. Just as the spring has brought the little tree to life, so I have come to bring you to life. Everything that before was dead will be made new and alive. It will be a transformation after the dead religion of the law.'

As Jesus moved through the streets of Jerusalem towards the Temple, people in the crowds jostled to catch a glimpse of him and his disciples. A few days earlier, Jesus had arrived in the holy city for the Passover, riding on a donkey, coming in what looked for all the world like a royal procession. People had cheered and cheered. They had taken off their cloaks and had laid them as a carpet in front of him. Then, after his arrival, Jesus had spent every day teaching the people. He had never been so popular with the crowds. Everybody wanted to hear him. Only the members of the ruling council at the Temple were angry. So far as they were concerned, Jesus was a threat to their power and to their religion. The chief priest, Caiaphas, had gone so far as to pass the sentence of death on him. But the Temple police did not dare to move against Jesus. Any attempt to arrest him would have caused a riot. So the Temple authorities did nothing directly.

As Jesus entered the Court of the Gentiles, the outer court of the Temple, he was greeted by a group of extremely excited men. They had with them a young woman, not much more than a girl. Her face was bleeding, her hair bedraggled, her clothes torn. The men were none too gentle with her and there was terror in her eyes. 'Master, Master,' shouted one of the men, 'we have caught a sinner in the very act. She has brought disgrace on herself, on her family and on the whole nation of Israel.' He grabbed the young woman and threw her forward so that she fell at Jesus' feet. 'We ask

A fig tree in winter

... and in summer

you, Master,' he said, 'to be her judge.' The men formed a large circle round Jesus and the young woman. Beyond the circle, Jesus could see the cruel, smiling faces of some of the Temple police. He guessed that they had something to do with what was going on.

'This must be a proper trial,' said the man. 'So I will present our case against her. Let it never be said that we, as men of Israel, lack justice.' The man was tall, quite young, with a muscular frame and sunburnt face. Jesus watched him intently. 'This woman,' said the man, 'is betrothed to a friend of mine, a respectable citizen of Bethlehem. He would have been here now, but he is too ashamed. You see, Master, we found this young woman in the arms of another man. There is no doubt that she is guilty. There are plenty of eye-witnesses.' He indicated the group of men and they assented and nodded.

Jesus looked at the men sadly. He knew what they wanted to do. The law of Moses, in the book Deuteronomy, laid down that an unfaithful wife should be strangled and that an unfaithful betrothed should be stoned to death. This group of men wanted to stone the young woman to death. Furthermore, they wanted Jesus' permission to do so. It was, in Jesus' time, against Roman law for the Jews to put anyone to death, but that would not stop the blood lust of a gang of men who had received permission from the most popular religious leader of the time. Jesus reflected that he had used

the parable of the fig tree to explain to people about new life found in his teachings and yet, so soon after, he was being asked to sentence a young woman to death. 'Come on, Master,' said the young woman's accuser, 'come on. No leader of Israel can deny the law of Moses.' Jesus noticed that many of the men had stones and rocks in their hands, ready to hurl at the young woman. He bent down and wrote some words in the dust. Then he straightened and looked around the circle of men. 'All right,' said Jesus, 'fulfil the law, but the first one to throw a stone must be someone who has never committed a sin in his life.' A look of astonishment came on each man's face. Each began to judge himself. Those who were carrying stones dropped them surreptitiously on the ground. One by one they began to move away. Jesus looked at the Temple police. They had stopped smiling. Lastly, the young woman's accuser left. 'Has no one condemned you?' said Jesus to the young woman. 'No,' she said. 'Then I will not condemn you either,' said Jesus. 'Go and sin no more.'

Understand your work

1 What was the meaning of the parable of the fig tree?

2 What had the young woman done and what did the law of Moses lay down as her punishment?

3 The New Testament does not tell us what Jesus wrote in the dust. What do you think he wrote?

The parable of the trees

Over a thousand years before Jesus saved the life of that young woman, the people of Israel learnt an important lesson about the weaknesses of human justice. There were no kings over Israel in those early days. The leaders were called judges and what was expected of them was that they could tell right from wrong. The greatest of these judges was Gideon. He had been asked if he would be king, but he had refused. 'The Lord will rule over you,' he said. For many years, the nation prospered under the guidance of Gideon.

Gideon had many wives and a prodigious number of children. There were sixty-nine sons! At least, there were seventy sons if one counted Jotham – which nobody did because he had a club foot and wrote poetry. (The only poetry considered worth writing at the time was war poetry.) There was, too, another son, but nobody mentioned him. His birth had cast a shadow on the house of Gideon because his mother was not an Israelite. She lived in Shechem and her son's name was Abimelech. The rest of the sons were hale and hearty young men who threw themselves enthusiastically into all the pleasures of life. Some liked hunting; others enjoyed foreign travel, while others, taking after their father, spent a great deal of time with the most beautiful women of the day.

The death of Gideon came as a shock. Everybody knew he was old but, somehow, the thought that he would actually die had not occurred to people. The day before his death, he was still passing judgements on the various problems brought before him. Then, during the night, he passed peacefully away in his sleep,

leaving the nation in a state of constitutional crisis. There was nobody to replace him; no man of obvious genius to take on the mantle of judge over Israel. The nation decided to turn to the sons of Gideon. Surely there would be one among them who had inherited his father's skills.

The sixty-nine sons were in Ophrah, preparing for their father's state funeral. As usual, they had forgotten to inform Jotham but Gideon's palace was crowded with the rest of them. The married sons had brought their wives and children. There were servants and maids, valets and messengers running in all directions. The sons themselves stood in small groups in the marble halls, joking and laughing, discussing what they were going to wear and what place each would have in the funeral procession through the streets of the city. When the high priest of Israel came, the sons gathered to listen to him in the spacious courtyard where cedar trees grew and peacocks strutted. When they all heard what he wanted, they all reacted with horror. 'Really,' said the eldest, 'what a cheek! You are asking me to give up my lifelong interest in chariot racing in order to become judge over Israel.' 'I couldn't imagine a more boring occupation than listening to other people's troubles every day,' said the second son. 'I was never cut out to be a judge,' said the third son. 'I can't even tell my right hand from my left.' 'The only thing I'm any good at', said the fourth son, 'is astrology.' Each son in turn was invited to be judge over Israel and each refused. The high priest was very upset.

There was one son of Gideon, though, who was dying to take his father's place. That was

Abimelech. He was still in Shechem with his mother. 'Am I not my father's son?' he said to her. 'Why then am I not invited to the funeral?' 'They have always hated us and kept us short of money,' said his mother, 'but the time has now come for revenge.' So Abimelech gathered together a gang of hoodlums and, travelling by night, he led them to the palace at Ophrah. They raided Gideon's palace in the early hours of the morning on the day of the funeral. They slaughtered every man, every woman, every child. Then, just before Gideon's funeral procession was about to begin, Abimelech went to the high priest. 'I am your new judge,' he said. By himself, he walked in the funeral cortege.

Abimelech's elevation to judge over Israel took place in Shechem. For Israel, it was shameful in the extreme. The political system was in ruins. The new judge cared nothing about right and wrong. Most people stayed away from the ceremony but Abimelech's thugs raised their fists in salute and his mother cried tears of joy as the high priest of Israel stepped forward to make him judge. Shechemites cheered. Children waved flags. Then . . . at the crucial moment, a shouting voice drew their attention. Everyone stopped and turned.

Outside the walls of the city stood Mount Gerizim, pointing like a needle into the sky. There, on the top of the mountain, stood Jotham, the brother everyone had forgotten. 'Listen to me, you men of Shechem,' he said, 'that God may listen to you. The trees once decided to anoint a king over the forest. "Reign over us," they said to the olive tree. But the olive replied, "Shall I stop producing my beautiful olive oil just so that I can rule over the trees?" Then the trees asked the fig tree. "Shall I cease to supply my succulent fruits just to become ruler of the forest?" replied the fig. So the trees asked the vine. "What a waste," said the vine. "My wine which gives men such pleasure will run dry." At last, the trees were obliged to accept the tyranny of a cruel and evil little bramble. "If you do not obey me," threatened the bramble, "I shall bring fire to burn down the whole forest." '

With these words, Jotham judged his sixty-nine brothers. They had shirked responsibility. He also judged Abimelech. He was to be made judge and he would rule by force, not by justice. Afterwards, Jotham was a fugitive and Israel suffered from Abimelech's power. There was no justice in Israel at that time.

Understand your work

1 What reason did Gideon give for refusing to become king over Israel?

2 Why did each of the sixty-nine brothers refuse the position of judge?

3 Explain Jotham's parable of the trees.

3

St. Nectan's equation

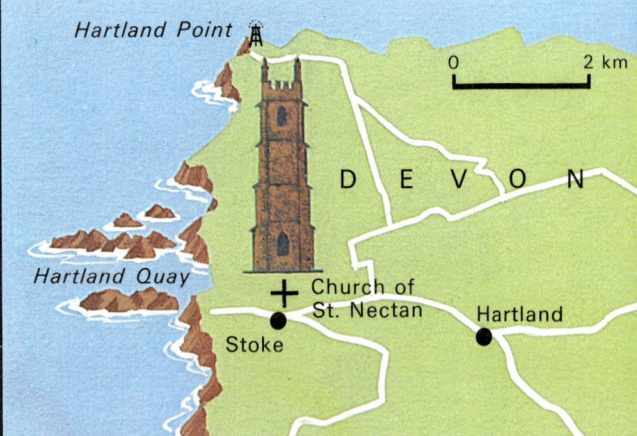

The church of St. Nectan is situated about half-way between Hartland village and the sea.

For centuries, this treacherous coast was a graveyard for ships.

A shipwreck brought all kinds of provisions to the poverty-stricken people of Hartland. Sometimes, they deliberately enticed ships onto the rocks.

The fourteenth-century church was designed with a great west tower, forty metres high. It could be seen far out at sea and warned the ships to keep away.

The architect also put a statue of the local holy man St. Nectan, half-way up the tower, gazing towards the village. The tower was for the sailors but the saint was for the villagers.

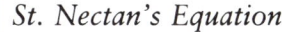

St. Nectan's Equation

Poor shipwreckers walked the green lanes
watching the stone saint
enshrined high on the granite tower.

Behind him, Atlantic rollers
threw cataclysms on the rocks,
sometimes carrying ships. The saint looked inland;

He looked lovingly at the village
a mile or so away, watched
the preparation of entrancing lights and shipwreck.

The sea was safer for his being there;
his tower traced the sky
and marked the sea-lanes, equalizing the chances.

Understand your work

1 Why are they described as 'poor shipwreckers'?

2 What was the purpose of the 'entrancing lights'?

3 Explain St. Nectan's equation in your own words.

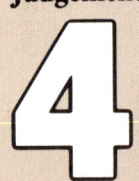

Judgement

4

The last judgement

This picture is in three parts because, during Lent when no pictures were displayed in the churches, the two side pictures, which were hinged, could be closed up covering the main picture. On the left hand side, souls are being taken into heaven. On the right hand side, souls are being taken down to hell. Notice that the entrance to hell is a dragon's mouth, wide open to receive the souls of the damned.

The last judgement. A French enamel made about 1500

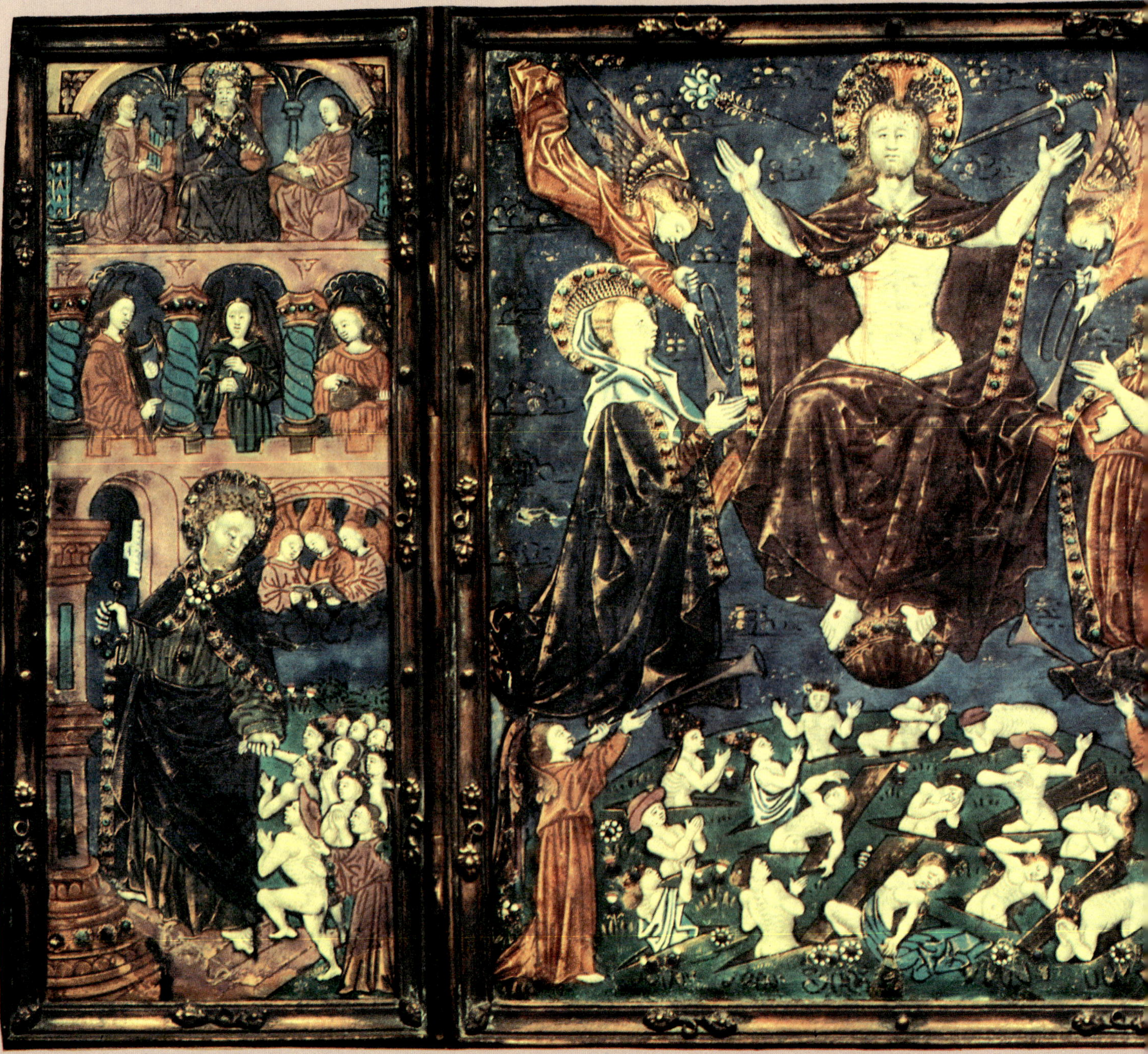

Understand your work

1 Read Matthew 25, 31–46. What ideas has the artist received from this passage.

2 There is a strange kind of perspective in this picture. Explain why some figures are much larger than others.

3 Study the hats worn by the little nude souls. What do the hats signify? What is there to suggest that the artist has had fun painting this picture?

5

Christian concepts of judgement

Jesus' encounter with the men who wanted to stone the young woman to death took place only days before he himself was arrested and condemned to crucifixion. That period after his triumphal entry into Jerusalem was almost entirely given over to teaching the crowds in the holy city. Jesus was in the Court of the Gentiles yet again on the day when the men brought their Passover lambs to the Temple for sacrifice. The court, usually so full of traders, was occupied that day by a great concourse of men with their lambs. The disciples Peter and John had bought a lamb and were in the crowd. Jesus was standing in the shadow of the covered way, surrounded by some of these men. 'Every day I have listened to you, Master,' one of them said, 'because your teachings are brilliant. But let me ask you something. You teach us about the kingdom of God and we are enlightened. But how will God treat all those people all over the world who have never heard of you or your teachings? Will God punish them for an ignorance they cannot help?' Jesus looked at the Temple itself, a small exquisite building surrounded by the courts. For centuries, the Jews had believed that the Temple was the home of the living God and that all other nations on earth were in complete ignorance of him. This was a surprising question from a Jew.

'When a shepherd goes home in the evening,' said Jesus, 'he divides up his flock. The sheep are far more valuable than the goats, so he separates them into a secure fold. In the same way, I will divide my human flock. To some, I will give nothing but praise. "When I was hungry," I will say, "you fed me. And when I was thirsty, you gave me drink." The others I will blame. "When I was starving, you refused me." And all those people to whom I will say these things will be extremely puzzled. "When did we feed you?" will ask those who have been praised. "When did we refuse you?" will ask the others. "We cannot remember doing such a thing." And I will give them their reply. "If you fed anyone who was hungry, you fed me and if you gave drink to anyone who was thirsty, you gave it to me." Does not that answer your question?' said Jesus. 'People who have treated others with compassion and generosity, whether they have heard my teachings or not, will be treated with compassion and generosity by God.'

This parable is found in St. Matthew's Gospel but, between the telling and the writing of the story, certain changes have taken place. The original question, to which the parable of the sheep and the goats was a reply, has been forgotten. So has the original meaning of the story. Jesus compared himself to a shepherd sorting out his flock at the end of the day. But St. Matthew's account is set at the end of time when Jesus, as a mighty judge, surrounded by angels, is seen coming in great glory to judge all mankind. St. Matthew, rather than Jesus, is the source of the painting of the Last Judgement which we have studied. It was not Jesus' purpose to show that he would be consigning people to heaven or hell. Rather, Jesus was teaching God's admiration for such qualities as compassion and generosity. Jesus did not portray himself as a final judge of mankind in the same sort of way that Jotham, on the top of Mount Gerizim, acted as the judge of his brothers.

Jesus' idea of his own role is shown, rather, in his encounter with the men who wanted to stone the young woman to death. It was quite usual for people in Jesus' day to approach religious leaders and to ask them to sit in judgement. The gospels tell us that this happened to Jesus many times. So it is not surprising that the men who wished to stone the young woman caught in adultery invited Jesus to act as judge and to pass sentence on her according to the law of Moses. But Jesus reacted by making each of those men judge himself. 'The first to throw a stone,' said Jesus, 'must be someone who has never committed a sin in his life.' It made each man realize that he was unable to throw the stone. Then Jesus refused to condemn the young woman. His only advice to her was, 'Go and sin no more.' She, too, had to work it out for herself.

Throughout the long history of Christianity, then, there have been two concepts of judgement. Many Christians have imagined heavenly courts to which men and women will be brought for judgement at the end of time. But Jesus himself taught that people must learn to judge themselves. The architect who placed the stone statue of St. Nectan on the great tower of the church at Hartland was encouraging precisely that sort of self-judgement. Anyone preparing an evil deed was meant to hesitate at the sight of him. Yet the saint himself is not sitting in judgement. He is a symbol of God's generosity and of his compassion for the villagers of Hartland, just as his tower has been a sign of God's care for generations of mariners.

Understand your work

1 Explain Jesus' parable of the sheep and the goats.

2 What differences were there between the parable as told by Jesus and the version written by St. Matthew?

3 What are the two concepts of judgement found in Christianity?

Work Section

Understand your work

1 Describe the difference between a fig tree in winter and a fig tree in spring.

2 Why did the men want Jesus to pass sentence on the young woman?

3 Why did the Israelites, in the early history of the nation, have judges to rule over them?

4 Why did Abimelech and his gang murder the brothers?

5 Why, in times gone by, did people in places like Hartland entice ships on to the rocks?

6 What was the purpose of the high tower at the church of St. Nectan?

7 A great many characters in the picture of the last judgement wear hats. What do they represent?

8 How does the artist show lack of respect for important people?

9 Why did a large number of men bring lambs to the Temple on the day when Jesus encountered the young woman caught in adultery?

10 In what way is the statue of St. Nectan both a warning and a sign of God's generosity and compassion?

Find out more

1 Read I Kings 3, 5–15 about King Solomon's accession to the throne of Israel.
   Answer the following questions:
   a What did Solomon say about his father, David?
   b What gift did Solomon ask for himself?
   c Why did this please God?
   d What did God promise?
   e In what way was Solomon's idea of leadership similar to that of an earlier Jewish political system? (Solomon was third king of Israel.)

2 Read I Kings 3, 16–28 and answer the following questions:
   a Explain the circumstances of the first dispute heard by Solomon.
   b How did Solomon decide which woman was right?
   c How did this prove to Solomon that God's promise had come true?

3 But if Gideon scandalized the Israelites by his relationship with the foreign woman at Shechem, that was nothing compared to Solomon's behaviour. Read I Kings 11, 1–13 and answer the following questions:
   a In what way did Solomon break the laws about marriage?
   b In what other ways was Solomon unfaithful to God?
   c What was God's judgement on Solomon?
   d How is the judgement reminiscent of the second commandment (Exodus 20, 5)?

4 The problem of wrongdoing among the early Christians worried the Church a great deal. They expected the Church to be a perfect society. Read Acts 4, 32–5, 11 and answer the following questions:
   a How did the members of the early Church organize their finances?
   b What did Ananias do?
   c In what way was it wrong?
   d What was the effect of the shock when he was found out?
   e What would a modern doctor say about his death?
   f What happened to Ananias' wife?
   g What was the effect of these events on the members of the Church?

5 So Ananias and Sapphira proved to the early Church that Christians sometimes did wrong and, soon after, the experiment in communism was discontinued for that reason. The leaders of the Church, however, continued to encourage the best possible behaviour among Christians. Read Romans 12, 9–21 and answer the following questions:
   a How were Christians to treat other people?
   b How were they to think of God?
   c How were they to treat members of the Church?
   d How were they to treat their enemies?
   e How were they to live in society?
   f Why should Christians never take revenge?
   g What was the basic principle of Christian living?

6 St. Caesarius, archbishop of Arles at the beginning of the sixth century, laid down a rule that the Te Deum should be said or sung at Morning Prayer. This is the first reference to one of the most famous hymns of the Church in which God is praised, the teachings of Christianity are summarised and God's mercy is sought:

   When thou hadst overcome the sharpness of death:
   thou didst open the kingdom of heaven to all
   believers.
   Thou sittest at the right hand of God: in the glory of
   the Father.
   We believe that thou shalt come: to be our Judge.

This is the way in which the Te Deum describes the role of Jesus Christ. It is a neat summary of New Testament teaching. Here are four biblical references – Matthew 25, 31; John 20, 19–23; Mark 16, 1–8; and Hebrews 1, 1–3. Match the references to statements in the part of the Te Deum which is quoted above.

7 John Donne (1572–1631) was a young man about town in London in the early 1590s. His love poems could not be published for fear of scandal. Later in his life, he was ordained a clergyman of the Church of England, became Dean of St. Paul's Cathedral and a celebrated preacher. Here is the first stanza of his poem 'A Hymne to God the Father':

Wilt thou forgive that sinne where I begunne,
Which is my sin, though it were done before?
Wilt thou forgive those sinnes, through which I
runne,
And do run still: though still I do deplore?
When thou hast done, thou hast not done,
For, I have more.

It is an effective description of a Christian sinner contemplating God's judgement on him. Study the words carefully befor answering the questions:

a His first question is whether God will forgive the sin that was 'done before'. Before what?
b What does he mean by 'those sinnes, though which I runne, and do run still'?
c How does he explain that although he does wrong, he despises himself for doing so?
d Look for the pun in the fifth line. How is it that God has both got and not got the poet?

8 In his *Screwtape Letters*, C. S. Lewis supplies us with the correspondence of an elderly devil, Screwtape, to his young nephew, Wormwood. Wormwood has been trying to prise a human 'patient' away from the power of the heavenly 'Enemy' and has had the assistance of a wartime air-raid. Screwtape, however, is not impressed with the results:

My dear Wormwood,
I sometimes wonder whether you think you have been sent into the world for your own amusement. I gather, not from your miserably inadequate report but from that of the Infernal Police, that the patient's behaviour during the first raid has been the worst possible. He has been very frightened and thinks himself a great coward and therefore feels no pride; but he has done everything his duty demanded and perhaps a bit more. Against this disaster all you can produce on the credit side is a burst of ill temper with a dog that tripped him up, some excessive cigarette smoking and the forgetting of a prayer. What is the use of whining to me about your difficulties? If you are proceeding on the Enemy's idea of 'justice' and suggesting that opportunities and intentions should be taken into account, then I am not sure that a charge of heresy does not lie against you. At any rate, you will soon find that the justice of Hell is purely realistic, and concerned only with results. Bring us back food, or be food yourself. . . .
Your affectionate uncle
Screwtape.

Answer the following questions:

a How has the human 'patient' behaved during the air-raid?
b Why does Screwtape call it the 'worst possible'?
c What bits of the 'patient's' behaviour can Wormwood claim to his credit?
d Why has Wormwood sent in a 'miserably inadequate report'?
e What does Screwtape say is the difference between a heavenly and a hellish idea of justice?

9 As the poet, Dylan Thomas, watched his father die, he felt very strongly that death itself was an injustice against which the old man should protest:

Do not go gentle into that good night,
Old age should burn and rave at close of day;
Rage, rage against the dying of the light.

Though wise men at their end know dark is right,
Because their words has forked no lightning they
Do not go gentle into that good night.

Good men, the last wave by, crying how bright
Their frail deeds might have danced in a green bay,
Rage, rage against the dying of the light.

Wild men who caught and sang the sun in flight,
And learn, too late, they grieved it on its way,
Do not go gentle into that good night.

Grave men, near death, who see with blinding sight
Blind eyes could rage like meteors and be gay,
Rage, rage against the dying of the light.

And you, my father, there on the sad height,
Curse, bless, me now with your fierce tears, I pray.
Do not go gentle into that good night.
Rage, rage against the dying of the light.

Answer the following questions:

a What does Dylan Thomas mean by the 'dying of the light'?
b Does it have a double meaning?
c How does the poet suggest the inevitability of death?
d How does the poet imagine that things might be different?
e Read Genesis 27, 27–30. How does Dylan Thomas use this reference at the end of his poem?

10 Here is an extract from T. J. Morris' *A Manual for Communicants*:

The more clearly we see God's glory
The more tawdry do our own sins become:
but
Assured of God's forgiveness, we move on
with confidence
from penitence to praise.

Answer the following questions:

a How does he explain that God's judgement is really our own judgement on ourselves?
b How does the assurance of God's forgiveness help Christians?
c Why does the Christian move on from penitence to praise?

1

Jesus' first sermon

Nazareth was an important Galilean village in Jesus' day. The houses were scattered among the olive groves on high sloping land to the west of Mount Tabor. Just below the village, the road wound through the mountains between Cana in the north and Jezreel in the south. The local people said that Nazareth afforded the best views in Israel. The synagogue dominated the village. It was an imposing square building surrounded by tall white columns. The best view of all was from the long stone steps which ran up to the entrance doors. Although this was a Jewish place of assembly, it had been designed in the Greek style fashionable at the time. No expense had been spared by the people of Nazareth whose own homes were humble enough. Inside the synagogue, there were more columns supporting the flat roof and, opposite the entrance doors, stood the large cupboard called the ark which contained the sacred scrolls of the scriptures. A curtain hung in front of the ark and there was a lectern for the reader and a seat for the preacher. The chief seats for important members of the synagogue were grouped around the ark. There was no segregation of men and women in Jesus' time.

The synagogue was a place of instruction and of assembly. It had traditionally been the responsibility of parents to teach the faith to their children but, as fathers became busier in their trades, they were grateful to the attendant, or hazzan as he was called, for his work as teacher at the synagogue school. Joseph, the carpenter, had been glad to send Jesus to his lessons. There he had learnt to read Hebrew and to recite the prayer known as the Shema: 'Hear, O Israel: The Lord our God, the Lord is one. . . .' The hazzan also assembled the villagers at Sabbaths and at festival times. He climbed onto the flat roof of the synagogue and blew three blasts on the trumpet to call the people together. At the assemblies he brought out the sacred scrolls from the ark, took off the beautiful embroidered cloths which covered them and ceremoniously presented them for reading. The scriptures had been written with immense care by professional scribes and they were the most valuable possessions of the synagogue.

The readers and the preacher at each assembly were chosen from among the villagers by the man known as the ruler of the synagogue. He had less to do than the hazzan but he was the most important person there, responsible for everything that went on.

The synagogue assemblies were simple affairs in Jesus' time. Elaborate ritual took place at the Temple in Jerusalem and, in the opinion of the villagers, that was the proper place for it. At least once during Jesus' childhood, the whole congregation had made the journey to the Temple for a festival. It was an occasion not easily forgotten by Joseph and Mary. At the end of the visit, they had set off for home assuming that Jesus was with the rest of the village children. They travelled a day's journey before realizing that he had been left behind in Jerusalem. Apart from this incident, Jesus' childhood in the village passed uneventfully enough. The early years of his adult life, too, were spent in the familiar surroundings. Since sons almost invariably followed the trades of their fathers in first-century Palestine, Jesus probably earned his living as a carpenter.

Everything changed when Jesus was about thirty years old. He made a solitary journey to the Jordan rift valley and was baptized by John the Baptist. Then he spent a long period in prayer, living like a hermit in the desert on the other side of the Jordan. For forty days, he wrestled with the problem of his own destiny. How could he serve Israel? In what way was he to serve mankind? During the course of his meditations, he sometimes imagined that he was arguing with the devil. Gradually, his mind clarified. He knew what he must do.

On the Sabbath after his return from the desert, Jesus attended the synagogue at Nazareth. Joseph, Mary, his brothers and sisters were there. The old hazzan who had instructed him at synagogue school welcomed him. The assembled villagers recited the Shema and parts of the psalms. One of the villagers read a portion of the Torah – the law of Moses. Then, at the invitation of the ruler of the synagogue, Jesus took the scroll of the Book of Isaiah. In the Hebrew which the hazzan

The remains of a Galilean synagogue from Jesus' time

had taught him, Jesus read:

> *The Spirit of the Lord is upon me, because he has anointed me to preach good news to the poor. He has sent me to proclaim release to the captives and recovering of sight to the blind, to set at liberty those who are oppressed, to proclaim the acceptable year of the Lord.*

Then Jesus rolled up the scroll and sat in the preacher's chair. Everyone waited with keen interest for his instruction on the scripture.

'Today,' said Jesus, 'this scripture has been fulfilled in your presence.' There was a stunned silence. 'Can you please explain?' said one of the men at last. 'That scripture can only be fulfilled with the coming of the Messiah – God's chosen one.' 'I know,' said Jesus. Immediately the villagers were gripped with anger and outrage. 'You are Joseph the carpenter's son,' they said. 'How dare you pretend to be anyone else?' 'Prophets', said Jesus, 'are never accepted where they were brought up. There are too many know-alls about.' At this, some of the villagers were so infuriated that they said that he should be stoned to death for blasphemy. Others wanted to throw him over a cliff. But while they were arguing, Jesus left the synagogue and hurried away.

Understand your work

1 Describe the synagogue at Nazareth.

2 Who were the two synagogue officials and what were their duties?

3 Why were the villagers at Nazareth angry with Jesus?

55

The Dead Sea scrolls

Since the earliest times, the scriptures were copied and re-copied by hand. The part of the scroll of Isaiah which Jesus read in the synagogue at Nazareth had been written by a professional scribe, copied probably on sheepskin or goatskin from an earlier version. The original had been written in the sixth century BC, but all copies as early as that had long disappeared in Jesus' time. A fascinating insight into the scrolls of Jesus' time was afforded in the late 1940s with the discovery of the Dead Sea scrolls.

The discovery took place in the early summer of 1947 when a Bedouin boy called Muhammad the Wolf was shepherding some goats on the

Qumran Cave 4

Remains of the Qumran settlement

western shore of the Dead Sea. In this strange area, over three hundred metres below sea level, there are cliffs broken with water courses, many of them honeycombed with caves. He noticed the entrance to a small cave and tossed a stone inside. To his surprise, he heard the sound of breaking pottery. He went back to the Bedouin tents and asked an older boy to help him investigate. The two boys squeezed inside the cave. There, they found a series of earthenware jars with bowl-like lids. They contained what looked like bundles of old rags. The boys took several of these bundles back to the Bedouin encampment. After they had removed the remains of the covering material, they found that they were left with long rolls of brown leather covered in parallel columns of handwriting. The writing meant nothing to the boys, but they believed their find could be valuable. When the Bedouins left the valley of the Dead Sea, the boys took the scrolls with them.

Despite the fact that the buying and selling of newly-discovered antiquities was strictly against the law at the time, five of these scrolls were eventually bought by the head of the Syrian monastery of St. Mark in Jerusalem. Rumour has it that he paid £50 for them. He was intrigued by what appeared to be very early Hebrew books. In February, 1948, he sent his scrolls to Dr John Trever of the American School of Oriental Research. At last the scrolls were in expert hands. Dr Trever had slides of early Hebrew manuscripts and he began by comparing the handwriting on the scrolls with the various scripts on the slides. Handwriting styles change a great deal from generation to generation and this was a way of dating the scrolls. What he discovered astonished him. There was a striking resemblance between the writing on the scrolls and that of the Nash Papyrus, a copy of the Ten Commandments written at about the time of Jesus. Dr Trever could hardly believe his eyes. It meant that the largest of the scrolls, a copy of the Book of Isaiah, was about eight hundred years earlier than any other copy of the book to survive to modern times. Such a copy could have been used by Jesus himself when he read from Isaiah to the congregation at Nazareth. When,

An earthenware jar from the caves

A Dead Sea scroll

a few months later, the head of the monastery sold his scrolls before moving to the United States, he is believed to have received £75,000 for them. It was still a low price.

Soon afterwards, every newspaper in the world carried such headlines as AMAZING DISCOVERY and BEDOUIN BOYS FIND TREASURE. It was not, however, a good time for such a discovery. In May, 1948, the Jewish struggle to set up the state of Israel erupted into war. Palestine was a dangerous place. At one famous press conference, bullets were whistling outside while an excited scholar was explaining about the scrolls to some very nervous newspaper reporters. The war made it impossible for scholars to visit the Dead Sea valley for themselves. It did not, however, stop the Bedouins. They realised that there was money be made and they lost no time in returning to the cave for more scrolls. Soon manuscripts, both genuine and forged, were changing hands for huge sums of money.

A great deal of the work of discovery in the years that followed was done by a combination of the Bedouins, an English archeologist, G. Lankester Harding, and a French priest, Roland de Vaux. Harding worked for the Jordanian government and succeeded in persuading the authorities to pay the Bedouins for their discoveries. From then on, he had

the co-operation of the Bedouins. He and Vaux visited the cave in 1949. By then, all the scrolls had gone but there were still some fragments of manuscript lying around. They also inspected the ruins of Qumran not far from the cave. They seemed to be the remains of a Roman fort. In 1951, Vaux made a search of more than two hundred caves in the area and found two more containing scrolls. In the same year, the Bedouins found four caves containing relics of the Bar-Kochba revolt against the Romans early in the second century. Then, in 1952, the Bedouins discovered the fourth cave which contained the main library of the Dead Sea. It came about because an old Bedouin was reminiscing. In his youth he had once followed a wounded partridge into a cave. Inside, he had seen an old lamp and some pottery. Following the old man's instructions, the Bedouins found a cave precariously high on the cliffs. It contained about four hundred manuscripts.

About the same time, Harding and Vaux inspected the Qumran ruins again. They made an important discovery. Underneath the remains of the Roman fort were the foundations of an ancient monastery. They found potsherds – bits of pottery on which scribes practised their writing. They found the remains of a long low slab at which scribes had sat while they wrote. They found the remains of the kiln in which the earthenware jars could have been fired. This was surely the source of the great religious library in the caves.

Understand your work

1   What were the scrolls like when they were first discovered?

2   Who first dated the scrolls and what method did he use?

3   Where did the Dead Sea library come from?

A weekend in Oxford

Statue of James I at the Bodleian Library

'I hope it's not going to be boring,' said Pete gloomily as they found themselves seats. 'At least it's a high speed train,' said Jim looking on the bright side. 'Don't forget to change at Reading,' fussed Jim's father, 'and give us a ring when you get there . . . and give our love to Uncle David.' Jim looked out at the rush and bustle of Paddington station. 'You'd better get off, Dad,' he said, 'otherwise you'll be changing at Reading as well.' Jim's father returned to the platform and, a few seconds later, the train was off. The two boys were going to Oxford for the weekend. It was towards the end of the long summer holiday and Jim's parents felt in need of a break. When Jim heard that he was expected to stay with his uncle, he had invited his friend Pete to accompany him. 'What's your uncle like?' Pete had asked. 'Oh, he's a weird professor type,' said Jim, 'but I don't suppose he'll bother with us.' Pete agreed to go but not without some misgivings.

The journey and their arrival in Oxford went smoothly enough. They found themselves sharing a spacious room high in the eaves of a tall Victorian house. Jim had expected his uncle to disappear back to his books as soon as he had seen the boys settled, but he showed no sign of doing so. 'As soon as you're ready,' he said, 'come down to the dining room. I'm sure you're famished and I want to discuss what we're going to do for the weekend.' He turned to leave, then looked back. 'I think you'd better call me David,' he said. Pete was horrified. 'I feel like going straight back home,' he said as soon as Jim's uncle had left them. 'I don't want to be dragged around the place by him!'

The following morning, two very reluctant boys followed David into the great paved courtyard of the Bodleian Library. 'There's James I,' said David, pointing at a statue on the wall half-way up the tower. 'Why has he got a book in each hand?' asked Pete. 'People in Oxford think it's a joke,' said David. 'When James was asked to give some books to the library, all he gave was a copy of his own writings. Later, when he had forgotten that he had given it, he gave a second copy.' David took the boys inside and up several flights of shallow stairs. 'I want you to see Duke Humphrey's library,' said David. 'It's the oldest part.' Suddenly, Jim and Pete completely forgot that they hadn't wanted to come. They found themselves in a fascinating world of leather-bound books. Beyond the barrier which separated them from the library itself, they could see people at their studies. The boys also admired the spectacular painted roof in white, blue, green and gold. 'It must be terribly old,' whispered Jim. 'Duke Humphrey was the youngest brother of King Henry V,' replied David. 'In his day, the library was in a church. The first library here was completed in 1490 and named after him because he gave so many manuscripts.'

David and the boys looked out of the window. They were practically on a level with James I's statue now. 'Books were so valuable when this library was opened,' said David, 'that the founders did not want them stored at ground level. It was less easy for thieves, rats and damp to get at books up here.' 'Then what did they do with the ground floor rooms?' asked Pete. 'They were the various schools of study,' said David, 'although they have been used for all kinds of things in their time. During the Civil War, for instance, the royalists used them for storing supplies for the troops and their horses. The tower was used for keeping gunpowder and shot.' The boys stared in fascination, trying to imagine the days when cavaliers strutted in and out of the ancient buildings.

'Here is a picture of Sir Thomas Bodley,' said David, pointing at a picture in the guide book. 'He was the man who got the library going as it is today. He had an adventurous life before marrying a wealthy wife. She died soon after the wedding, leaving him rich and with time on his hands. He came to Oxford in 1597 and found Duke Humphrey's library in terrible condition. Of the six hundred manuscripts that the duke had given, twenty remained. The parchment on which they had been written was also useful for making candles and many of them were obtained by the merchants of Oxford for that purpose.' 'You mean to say that a book which someone had taken ages to write by hand was turned into candles?' said Pete, horrified. 'Some of the monks took years with their books,' said David. He took the boys down to ground level again and they visited the exhibition room. There, they saw books from many different periods. 'I like the old handwritten ones,' said Jim, 'with all that gold and red decoration.' 'Doesn't the print on the earliest printed books look just like handwriting?' commented Pete. 'That's because the early printers copied handwriting,' said David. 'Print only later developed a style of its own.' Later, David and the boys emerged from the library. 'Bodley himself had some peculiar ideas from our

Picture of Sir Thomas Bodley by Nicholas Hilliard

point of view,' said David. 'He lived in the age of Shakespeare but he was not the least interested in buying copies of his plays. People would pay a small fortune now for the books Bodley didn't bother to collect.' 'What interested him if it wasn't plays?' asked Jim. 'Religion,' said David. 'He was a keen protestant and believed that his library would help in the struggles against the Roman Catholic Church. One of the first things he did was to get a list of books banned by Rome so that he could buy them for this library.' 'Last term', said Jim, 'we learnt about the Dead Sea Scrolls in school. That was a religious library.' 'So was this to start with,' said David.

'It's school at the end of next week,' said Pete as the two boys settled themselves into the train that would take them back to London. 'I hate education,' said Jim, 'It's so boring.' 'The nice thing about your Uncle David', said Pete, 'was that he didn't try to educate us.'

Duke Humphrey's Library

Understand your work

1 Why did the two boys dislike the idea of being taken round Oxford by David?

2 Why were the books at the Bodleian stored above ground floor level and what use was made of the ground floor?

3 Why did Sir Thomas Bodley use a list of books banned by the Roman Catholic Church as a shopping list for the library?

Passing on the message

From the earliest times, religion and communication have gone together. A primitive man dipped his fingers into a mixture of blood and sand in order to depict this bison. He believed that his picture would give him magical powers over the animal.

By Jesus' day, the teachings of prophets like Isaiah were available in the synagogue at Nazareth because they had been written by professional scribes.

The ancient Egyptians went on to develop a form of writing based on pictures. It was deciphered in 1822 by Jean Francois Campollion. Most surviving Egyptian literature is about their religion.

The scribes at Qumran in Jesus' day laboriously copied out the books of the Old Testament. They also produced a literature about their own religious ideas, centred on a leader whom they called 'The Teacher of Righteousness'.

Their pens were made out of hollow reeds cut from the nearby marshes and two of their inkwells have survived, one of bronze, the other of clay. Their ink was made out of soot, lamp oil, gelatin of donkey skin, and musk. (The musk was to neutralize the smell of the gelatin.)

The alternative to papyrus was sheepskin or goatskin. The wool or hair side of the skin was cleaned off and scraped. Then the skin was soaked in a solution containing tannic acid which stopped it from going hard and brittle. Finally, many skins were carefully sown together to make the long strips of material on which the scribes wrote.

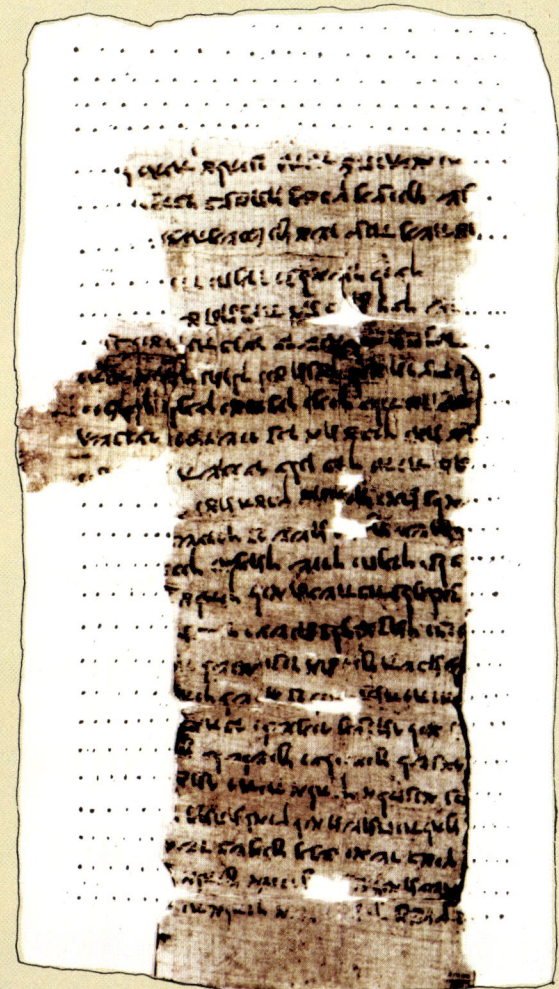

All early books were in scroll form. Even today, modern synagogues continue to have their scriptures written in this fashion. The reader holds the book by the handles and twists them to change the pages. The Dead Sea scrolls were meant to be read in this fashion and so was the scroll read by Jesus in the synagogue at Nazareth.

A great deal of early writing was on papyrus. It was made by laying thin stips of the pith of the papyrus plant in rows. Then further strips were added, running at right angles to the original ones. The material was then pressed, dried and polished. Finally, the papyrus squares were glued together to make long rolls. The illustration is of the Nash Papyrus, used by Dr John Trever to date the Dead Sea scrolls.

Books produced in Europe in the Middle Ages certainly looked very different from the scrolls of Jesus' time. They were quired, sown and bound like modern books. Yet the basic method was the same. Books were still being copied by hand on to animal skins. Anyone wishing to buy a book in Oxford in 1450, for instance, would borrow a copy from Duke Humphrey's library, housed in the church of St. Mary the Virgin. He would then pay one of the professional penmen who had shops on Catte Street, along the east wall of the church, to copy the book out.

Many of the Mediaeval copyists were monks, adding books to the monastery libraries. They usually wrote with a trimmed goose quill, the favourite writing implement in Europe for centuries. They decorated their manuscripts with gold leaf and many colours.

This is the work of Stephen Doddesham, monk of the Charterhouse of Sheen. It is a copy of part of Nicholas Love's 'The myrrour of the blessed lif of Ihesu Crist'. Just as the writings of the ancient Egyptians and the scribes of Jesus' day were largely to do with religion, so was the vast majority of the manuscripts of the Middle Ages.

Everything changed with the beginning of printing. Metal type, in mirror writing, was organized into pages, fixed into a wooden frame, painted with ink and pressed against a sheet of paper. It took a long time to make the type and to assemble it but, once the work was done, any number of copies could be made. It was a great step forward.

The device used to press the type against the paper was called a press because it was designed on the same principle as the presses used to squeeze juice out of grapes in preparation for making wine. Early printing was very similar in appearance to the handwriting of the time.

The art of paper-making spread throughout Europe at about the time when printing was beginning to make books much cheaper. Paper was made by rotting and pounding linen rags, then spreading the mixture on a kind of tray with a base made of brass wires. It is possible to see the traces of these wires if early paper is held up to the light. Water marks were made by adding designs in the wire. The arrival of paper helped to further reduce the cost of books.

There have been many improvements in communication since the invention of printing. Today, paper is made out of wood and turned out in gigantic rolls. Words can be typed on to a television screen, read, corrected and stored on magnetic tape, ready to be printed at the press of a button. We have come a long way since primitive man dipped his fingers into a mixture of blood and sand in order to depict a bison.

As more and more people had printed books and learned to read them, there was a great demand for the Bible in a language they could understand. The Bible had originally been translated from Greek and Hebrew into Latin by St. Jerome in the fourth century. For over a thousand years, people learned about the Bible from the clergy rather than at first hand. Now that they could read, they wanted printed Bibles in English. It took over a century of successive translations before, in 1611, the Authorized Version was published. It is still used in many churches today.

Understand your work

1 Describe how the monks at Qumran produced the Dead Sea scrolls.

2 How would one obtain a book in Mediaeval Oxford?

3 Can you read Stephen Doddesham's manuscript. Attempt to write it out.

Johann Gutenberg's invention

Johann Gutenberg was born in Mainz in Germany sometime around the year 1400. He was a goldsmith by trade, specializing in the making of mirrors and in gem cutting. But while Gutenberg earned his living in this way, his real interests lay elsewhere. In his early years, he travelled extensively around Europe. Then, in 1430, he settled in Strasbourg. The first clues to his real interests came in 1438 when he entered into a contract with three other partners. They were Hans Riffe, Andreas Heilman and Andreas Dritzehn. The four men were working together on a project which Gutenberg wished to keep secret. One of the terms of the contract, however, was that if one of the partners should die, his heirs should not be taken into the company but should, instead, be compensated with money. At Christmas, 1438, Dritzehn died. His heirs refused the money which was offered and brought a case against Gutenberg, claiming part of the company. Their claim failed but, in the process, some of Gutenberg's activities were revealed. Hans Dünne, a goldsmith, told the court that he had sold Gutenberg a hundred guilders worth of various metals in 1436. Also, a carpenter called Conrad Saspack revealed that he was involved in the building of a device rather like a wine press. Anyone living at the time could guess what Gutenberg was doing. One of the greatest needs of the time was that someone should develop a method of printing.

A printer's matrix and letter

Gutenberg's method, devised sometime in the 1430s, has been used to a large extent ever since. Being a goldsmith, he was skilled in the cutting of metal with a considerable degree of precision. He began by cutting the whole alphabet, both capital and lower case, in mirror writing on the ends of a series of steel punches. For the design of the letters, he chose the best handwriting of the time. Then he hammered the punches into square copper bars, sinking the shapes of the letters into the copper. Each copper bar, in turn, was fitted into a mould and a hot mixture of lead and tin was poured in. When this had cooled and hardened, it was a perfect copy of the original letter on the punch. In this way, Gutenberg overcame one of the main problems of printing. He could produce as many copies of a letter as he wanted. The type which he produced by this method was then arranged into words and spaces on a flat tray, called a galley. When sufficient pages of print had been made up, they were locked into a wooden frame, called a chase. Ink was painted on to the face of the mirror writing. Then, in the press, a sheet of paper was impressed on to the type producing a readable copy.

Gutenberg's printing system had one great advantage over handwriting. Once a page of type had been set up, any number of copies could be produced. The only extra cost was ink and paper. But Gutenberg's method also had one great disadvantage. A printer had to spend a great deal of money on type, paper and the pay of employees before a single copy of a book could be produced. Setting it all up was very expensive. In 1448, Gutenberg was back in Mainz, borrowing money from a wealthy financier called Johann Fust. He offered Fust his tools and his printing equipment as security for a loan of eight hundred guilders. Two years later, Fust lent a further eight hundred guilders in return for a partnership. Soon after, there was a clash between the two men. Gutenberg was a perfectionist. It was not enough to be the father of European printing. He wanted to print with the same kind of artistry as that shown by the writers of Mediaeval illuminated manuscripts. Fust, on the other hand, wanted a quick return on his

The Gutenberg Bible

money. He brought a case against Gutenberg for the recovery of his loans on November 6th, 1455. Gutenberg was ordered to pay him two thousand and twenty six guilders. When Gutenberg was unable to pay, Fust got possession of all his print and his printing press.

Before his ruin at Fust's hands, Gutenberg had succeded in printing one book. The Gutenberg Bible was the first printed book in Europe. It was, undoubtedly, a tremendous undertaking for so new a craft as printing. It required the use of six printing presses, a great deal of manpower and probably took the best part of a year to produce. It was a measure of Gutenberg's ambition that he should begin with such a task. Yet it was not surprising. He was following in the tradition of all those people, throughout history, who have gone to great pains for the sake of religious writings. In Jesus' day, there were scrolls in all the synagogues, laboriously handwritten by scribes. In his time, too,

there was the great Dead Sea library. Centuries later, monks were producing superb illuminated manuscripts and penmen, like those in Catte Street, Oxford, in the fifteenth century, continued to copy religious works. After Gutenberg, the tradition continued. In the first two centuries of printing, far more religious books were published than any other kind and, in Oxford, Sir Thomas Bodley set up his library with religion in mind. Nowadays, the Bodleian is a great university library, visited by scholars from all over the world. Much has changed since Bodley's time yet, even today, the Bible is still a best seller.

Understand your work

1 What method did Gutenberg devise for making type?

2 How did Gutenberg come to be ruined just as success was in sight?

3 Why was the first printed book in Europe a Bible?

Work Section

Understand your work

1 What were the scrolls of the scriptures like and where were they kept in the synagogue?

2 Jesus read part of the prophecy of Isaiah when he visited the synagogue at Nazareth. What did the Jews believe that reading was about?

3 Who were the people responsible for finding further caves near the Dead Sea? What else did they find?

4 How did the discovery of the fourth cave come about?

5 Why was the Bodleian originally a religious library?

6 Why do people in Oxford regard the statue of James I as a joke?

7 How were books made in 1450?

8 How was paper made at the time of the invention of printing?

9 What is meant by the words 'galley' and 'chase'?

10 What was Gutenberg's method of printing?

Correct these statements

1 Every synagogue had a model of Noah's ark.

2 Jesus spent forty days being baptized in the Jordan.

3 Muhammad the Wolf was an expert in early Hebrew manuscripts.

4 The earthenware jars which contained the Dead Sea scrolls were made out of potsherds.

5 Duke Humphrey gave the Dead Sea scrolls to the Bodleian Library.

6 Sir Thomas Bodley was a cavalier who fought in the War of the Roses.

7 The goose quill was an essential part of printing equipment.

8 Stephen Doddesham painted animals on the walls of his cave.

9 Gutenberg was a carpenter who had wine presses.

10 Johann Fust stole the Gutenberg Bible.

Find out more

1 The discovery of the Dead Sea scrolls was undoubtedly the most remarkable find in the history of religious literature. It was by no means, however, the first of such finds. Read 2 Kings 22, 1–13 and answer the following questions:

  a Who was king in Jerusalem at the time?

  b How old was he when he sent his secretary to the Temple?

  c What was Shaphan to do?

  d Why did the king say that there was no need for accounts from the workmen?

  e What was discovered during the repairs?

  f What did Shaphan do with the discovery?

  g How did the king react?

2 It is not surprising that a discovery of this kind was made in the Temple in Josiah's time (he reigned 640–609 BC). Read, for instance, 1 Samuel 10, 25 (c 1075 BC) and answer the following questions:

  a Who wrote a book about the rights and duties of kingship?

  b What did he do with it?

3 Solomon's Temple (c 950 BC) had not, of course been built in Samuel's time. The holy place of the Jews was at Shiloh, twelve miles south of Shechem. It would, however, have been quite natural for Samuel's writings, together with other holy objects at Shiloh to have been transferred to the Temple. Read I Kings 8, 1–21 and answer the following questions:

  a What was the most holy object to be transferred to the Temple?

  b What else did they bring?

  c Where did they place the ark of the covenant?

  d What was inside the ark?

  e Why were there no windows in the holy of holies?

  f What did Solomon say about his father, David?

  g What did he say about himself?

4 The effect of the discovery in the Temple makes us suspect that what was found was part of the book Deuteronomy. Read II Kings 23, 21–24 and answer the following questions:

  a What Jewish festival was observed differently as a result?

  b How long was it, according to II Kings, since the festival had been properly celebrated?

  c What other reforms happened as a result?

5 Read Deuteronomy 13, 1–3 and answer the following questions:

  a What connection do you see between this passage and the reforms of II Kings?

  b How does the author of Deuteronomy explain the existence of other religions and how are the Jews to treat them?

6 Sacred writings, then, can affect people long after the author has written them. The anonymous author of Deuteronomy had hidden his writings in the Temple and, eventually, they had a great impact on King Josiah and his subjects. The scribes who copied the Dead Sea scrolls have had a quite different kind of impact on modern scholarship. It is interesting, however, to see how one of the writers of the Bible set about his task.

Read Luke 1, 1–4 and answer the following questions:

a What does Luke say about sacred writings in his time?

b How does he describe the original disciples and apostles?

c What is Luke's own intention?

d To whom is the gospel dedicated?

7 After New Testament times, the next task to face the Church was the formulation of Christian rules about belief and behaviour. Jesus had supplied his followers with the principles, but the Christians, under the guidance of the Holy Spirit, had to work out the practice for themselves. The Apostles' Creed, for instance, is an early Christian document making a list of beliefs. Read the Creed and answer the following questions:

a What part of the creed refers to God as he is described in the Old Testament?

b What part is a summary of the gospels?

c What does the Creed say about the Church itself?

8 Most of the rules for belief and the running of the Church were worked out in the first few centuries and the documents of the early Church are of great importance to all Christians. A second set of important documents appeared, however, at the Reformation in the sixteenth century when the western church fragmented. There were, for instance, the decrees of the Council of Trent, setting out the Roman Catholic position, and, in England, the Thirty-nine Articles which in 1571 defined the beliefs of the Church of England. There is a copy at the end of the Book of Common Prayer. Read Article VI and answer the following questions:

a What does the article say about Holy Scripture?

b What rule does the article lay down for judging documents (the Creed for instance) which are not in the Bible?

c What does the article say about the books the authority of which is in doubt?

9 Apart from original writings, the work of the Church has been greatly affected by the translators. The Old Testament was originally written in Hebrew. There was, however, an early Greek translation called the Septuagint. (The books in doubt mentioned in the last question appear in the Septuagint but not in the Hebrew Bible.) The New Testament was written in Greek. In the fourth century, St. Jerome (also mentioned in Article VI) produced a Latin version of the Bible called the Vulgate. In English, the Authorized Version, published in 1611, has had a profound effect on our language and culture. Read the dedicatory letter at the beginning of the Authorized Version and answer the following questions:

a Why is the Authorized Version sometimes called the King James Bible?

b Who is compared to a western star and who to the sun?

c What is the 'inestimable treasure which excelleth all riches'?

d What sources do the translators say they have used for the Authorized Version?

There is, in the dedicatory letter, a disparaging reference to 'Popish persons'. What happened on November 5th, 1605?

10 Since 1611, there have been many discoveries, like the Dead Sea scrolls, which have affected our knowledge of the Bible. As a result, the twentieth century in particular has seen a host of new translations of the Bible. The translation which has been used throughout these lessons is the Revised Standard Version which, although it originates in America, has combined the qualities of the Authorized Version with the results of modern scholarship. Read the last paragraph of the preface and answer the following questions:

a What does the preface say about the Bible as a historical document?

b What does it say about the Bible as literature?

c What does it say about God?

d What is said about Jesus?

e What does it say about the teachings of the Bible and the work of translators?

f What is the purpose of the Revised Standard Version?

Use your imagination

1 Describe a conducted tour of a typical synagogue in Jesus' time.

2 Tell the story of the visit to the Temple from Jesus' point of view. (Luke 2, 41–52)

3 Write Muhammad the Wolf's own account of the discovery of the Dead Sea scrolls.

4 Write a short play in which Harding and Vaux are inspecting the ruins of Qumran.

5 Describe a visit to a modern religious bookshop. What kinds of books are on sale?

6 Write a short story in which Pete and David visit a monastery.

7 Describe a visit to a penman's shop in Oxford before the invention of printing.

8 Write a short conversation between a scribe in Jesus' time and a modern printer.

9 Make a painting of Gutenberg's workshop.

10 Compose a letter written by Gutenberg to Johann Fust, pleading with him not to make him bankrupt.

The Beatitudes

Seeing the crowds, he went up on the mountain, and when he sat down his disciples came to him. And he opened his mouth and taught them, saying:

'Blessed are the poor in spirit, for theirs is the kingdom of heaven.

'Blessed are the meek, for they shall inherit the earth.

'Blessed are those that mourn, for they shall be comforted.

'Blessed are those who hunger and thirst for righteousness, for they shall be satisfied.

'Blessed are the merciful, for they shall obtain mercy.

'Blessed are the peacemakers, for they shall be called sons of God.

'Blessed are those who are persecuted for righteousness' sake, for theirs is the kingdom of heaven.

'Blessed are you when men revile you and persecute you and utter all kinds of evil against you falsely on my account. Rejoice and be glad, for your reward is great in heaven, for so men persecuted the prophets who were before you.'

Understand your work

1 In what ways could the psalmist who wrote Psalm 104 be described as meek?

2 How did the king's treasurer in Jesus' parable fail to be merciful?

3 Give Jesus' final advice to his disciples in your own words.

'Blessed are the pure in heart, for they shall see God.

Laws and principles

According to St. Matthew's Gospel, Jesus' Sermon on the Mount began with the Beatitudes. There is a similar account of such a sermon in St. Luke's Gospel which, because the setting is different, is called the Sermon on the Plain. Probably neither version of this sermon was preached in the way described in the gospels. During the period when stories of Jesus were passed on by word of mouth, it was natural for people to make collections of his sayings. There is evidence that some of these collections were written down. A number of papyrus manuscripts were found in 1945, for instance, buried in a jar in the pagan cemetery at Nag Hammadi in Egypt. Among them was a document called the Gospel of Thomas. It is not a gospel but a collection of Jesus' sayings, dated about 150 AD. That particular collection is dated later than the gospels of the New Testament but scholars believe that both Matthew and Luke possessed a copy of a similar collection of sayings and used it as one of the sources of their gospels. No copy has survived. Scholars call it 'Q'. It is likely that 'Q' was the source of the Beatitudes both in St. Matthew's Gospel and in St. Luke's.

A page of the Gospel of Thomas

The Beatitudes are in the style of Hebrew poetry, especially the psalms. They are reminiscent, in particular, of Psalm 37:

But the meek-spirited shall possess the earth: and shall be refreshed in the multitude of peace.

and

The righteous shall inherit the land: and dwell therein for ever.

By setting the sermon on the mountain, St. Matthew was also reminding his readers of the Ten Commandments which had been given by God to Moses on the top of Mount Sinai. Eight of the Ten Commandments begin with the words, 'you shall not', warning people against such evils as the worship of idols, murder and theft. But instead of supplying laws, as Moses had done, Jesus laid down principles by which his followers were to live. The laws were negative, but the principles were positive, encouraging a particular attitude to life. In his introduction to the Sermon on the Mount, St. Matthew uses the word 'disciples' for the first time in his gospel. Only through these teachings can men be made Jesus' disciples.

Jesus turns upside down the usual ideas about human happiness. The 'poor in spirit' are people who don't consider themselves at all and, consequently, concentrate the whole of their lives on God:

Therefore do not be anxious, saying, 'What shall we eat?' or 'What shall we drink?' or 'What shall we wear?' For the Gentiles seek all these things; and your heavenly Father knows that you need them all. But seek first his kingdom and his righteousness, and all these things will be yours as well.

'Those who mourn' are people who realize the existence of evil and struggle to put matters right. The meek, not the strong, inherit the earth. The purpose of life is to seek goodness, purity and

A nineteenth-century stained-glass window showing the
Sermon on the Mount

peace. For the sake of such things, Jesus' followers
will gladly suffer any persecution. In St. Luke's
version, Jesus goes on to warn people who behave
in the opposite manner. The rich and well-fed are
so arrogant that God means nothing to them. Men
may speak well of them, but God will not reward
them.

The principles which Jesus laid down for his
disciples in the Beatitudes did not give them specific
instructions on how they should behave. The law of
Moses had concerned itself to a large extent with
crimes which did actual harm, but Jesus was much
more concerned with what went on in a person's
mind:

> You have heard that it was said to the men of
> old, 'You shall not kill; and whoever kills shall
> be liable to judgement.' But I say to you that
> every one who is angry with his brother shall
> be liable to judgement. . . .

The word 'peacemakers' does not properly translate
what Jesus meant. Jesus spoke Aramaic but, as he

showed when he visited the synagogue at Nazareth,
he also read Hebrew. The Hebrew word for peace
is 'shālôm'. It is used as a greeting. To wish
somebody 'shālôm' is to welcome and to desire
well-being for that person. It is open-hearted,
generous and joyful. It is the opposite to anger.

Since Jesus supplied principles rather than
rules, they have been interpreted in many different
ways during the course of the long history of
Christianity. He did not tell his followers how to
run a church nor did he supply a neat system of
belief. All that was left for his disciples to work out
for themselves.

Understand your work

1 What evidence is there that collections of Jesus' sayings
were written in the early period of Christianity?

2 In what ways could St. Simeon Stylites be described as
'poor in spirit'?

3 In what ways was St. Nectan's statue a symbol of the
peacemakers?

3

Faustus, an Elizabethan performance

Sometimes Will Smart and his wife, Maria, went to the theatre. Not everybody in Elizabethan London approved. The Puritans insisted that sermons were the only entertainment. They called the theatres heathenish and were for ever campaigning to get them closed. But Will was no Puritan. He and Maria lodged in a tall, narrow, timber-framed house quite near to the printer's workshop where Will was employed. A quarter of an hour's walk away, on Golden Lane, was the newly-built Fortune Theatre. It was just outside the city wall, near the Cripplegate. People flocked there from all over the city, particularly when the famous actor, Ned Alleyn, was treading the boards. Some people reckoned him the finest actor in London. One afternoon in late summer, in the year 1601, Will and Maria went to see him play Doctor Faustus.

They made a point of arriving early. A full hour before the theatre bell was due to be rung, signalling the beginning of a performance, Will paid for admission and they pushed their way into the central courtyard around which the theatre was built. He could not afford to pay for the seats which occupied a series of balconies right round. So they had come early in the hope of being able to stand near the stage. The place was already almost half full of richly dressed men and women. The long dresses of the women were gold and red, green and orange and the men wore short cloaks and neat doublet and hose. Will was lucky to find a corner of the stage for himself and Maria. The theatre was almost circular, with a roof over the seats and over the big stage which projected into the courtyard. Maria looked up. The courtyard was open to the sky but, fortunately, there was no sign of rain. She hated having fine clothes spoilt by the rain.

At last, the bell was rung and the flag was flown to show that a performance was in progress. Will gave a little shudder of anticipation. Kit Marlowe, the author of the play, had had a bad reputation. Eight years earlier, he had been a wanted man, suspected of blasphemy and heresy. But Marlowe had cheated justice. Before he could be arrested, he had been killed in a tavern brawl. Will had heard that his play was about a man who had sold his soul to the devil. Perhaps that's what Marlowe had done. Will may have been no Puritan but he firmly believed in the power of the devil. He had heard many sermons describing the agonies of lost souls burning for ever in hell. He had seen many paintings of devils with tridents, stoking the everlasting fires.

Practically as soon as the play had begun, a curtain at the back of the stage was drawn back to reveal Doctor John Faustus, scholar of Wittenberg. Very little scenery was used in the Elizabethan theatre but he had a desk, a chair and piles of leather-bound volumes. Faustus, played impressively by Alleyn, did not confine himself to the area beyond the curtain but wandered around the main stage as he talked about each of his books in turn. He knew them all and was bored by them. Then he came to a book about the occult and magical arts. That intrigued him. He began to wonder what diabolical mysteries he could discover. Within a short time, Faustus had conjured up a devil called Mephostophilis and had drawn up a contract with him, written in his own blood. Faustus was to have twenty-four years of life during which the devils would serve him. After that, his soul would be consigned to hell.

Although the play was a tragedy about the way in which Faustus condemned himself to everlasting torment, there were many scenes which had the audience roaring with laughter. Marlowe had included a clown and several very funny servants in his play. Will soon noticed that the more the audience laughed, the sadder the fate of Faustus himself appeared. The twenty-four years promised to him seemed very long at first but they passed with increasing rapidity. And Faustus became more and more desperate. He received very little for the loss of his soul. He was entertained by a performance of the Seven Deadly sins; he was taken on a tour of foreign countries; he organized a royal command performance for the German Emperor and he supplied a duchess with grapes when they were out of season. It was not much to show.

As the play progressed, Will began to realize that Marlowe had suggested an idea of hell quite different from that taught in church. God did not abandon Faustus. Mephostophilis kept on insisting that there was no going back on the contract, but Faustus was haunted by a good angel. Faustus knew that God would forgive him. But he also knew that he was incapable of receiving forgiveness:

> *Second scholar*   Yet, Faustus, call on God.
> *Faustus*   On God, whom Faustus hath adjured? On God, whom Faustus hath blasphemed? Oh, my God, I would weep but the devil draws in my tears. Gush forth blood instead of tears, yea, life and soul. Oh, he stays my tongue. I would lift up my hands, but see, they hold them, they hold them.
> *All*   Who, Faustus?
> *Faustus*   Why, Lucifer and Mephostophilis.

The devils were really in Faustus' mind. The real hell was a state of mind in which a human being could not accept God. It did not fit in with the religious ideas of the time but it taught a message very close to Jesus' Beatitudes. The 'poor in spirit' were blessed because they concentrated their lives on God. The kingdom of heaven belonged to them. But Faustus was already in hell, his spirit trapped by evil.

'Methinks', said Will to Maria as they walked back into the city of London, 'that Master Marlowe taught religion better than most preachers.' She nodded in agreement.

Understand your work

1 Why did Faustus become more and more desperate as the play progressed?

2 What was Marlowe's play really saying about hell?

3 Why did Will reckon that Marlowe taught religion better than most preachers?

Edward Alleyn, 1566-1626

Towards the end of the reign of Elizabeth I, a generation of fine playwrights appeared on the London scene. William Shakespeare was the greatest but there were many others. Christopher Marlowe could well have developed into a playwright to rival Shakespeare himself. He had spent six years at Cambridge University, studying to become a clergyman but, at the same time, he appears to have been a secret agent for the government. His undercover activities may explain why, at the age of twenty-nine, he was murdered during a fight in a Deptford tavern. His murderer, Ingram Frizar, also had connections with the secret service and it arouses suspicion that, one month after the murder, he was given a free pardon. Certainly, the English theatre was robbed of a playwright of genius. Playwrights like Shakespeare, Marlowe and the rest wrote plays suitable for the circular, open-air theatres which were built at various places just outside the walls of London. Theatres were not built in the city because the companies wished to avoid control by the civic authorities.

To complement the playwrights and the theatres, there appeared also many fine actors. Shakespeare himself acted for a company called the Chamberlain's Men at the Globe Theatre on Bankside. But the two most famous actors of the day were Richard Burbage and Edward Alleyn. Burbage belonged to the same company as Shakespeare and acted in his plays. Alleyn, on the other hand, was famous for his performances in the four plays written by Christopher Marlowe. He belonged to the Lord Admiral's Company and, in 1592, he married Joan Woodward, stepdaughter of Philip Henslowe, owner of the Rose Theatre. In 1600, in partnership with Henslowe, Alleyn was responsible for building the Fortune Theatre on Golden Lane, near the Cripplegate. Apart from the theatre, he also took an interest in other forms of entertainment popular at the time. He was part owner of a baiting house in the Paris Garden, Southwick. There, dangerous animals such as bulls and bears were chained, then tormented into a fury for the amusement of the audience. Sometimes

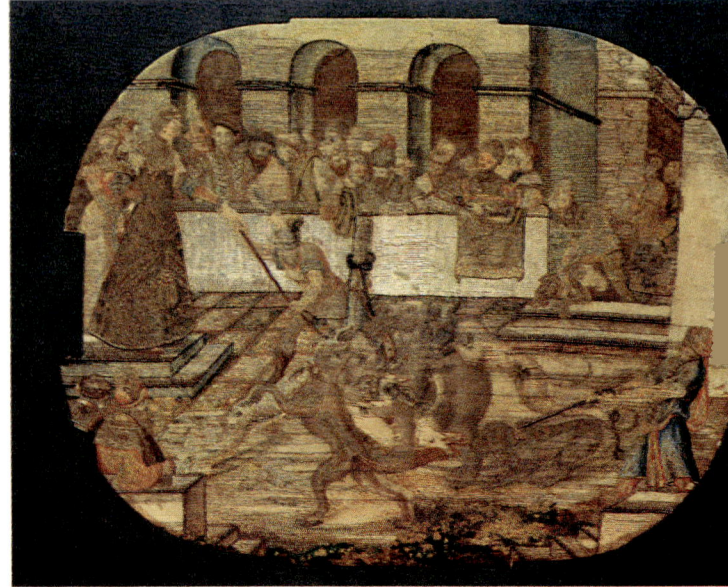

A late sixteenth-century embroidery showing bear-baiting

Alleyn himself took part in the entertainment. One account, written at the time, tells of the part played by Alleyn in the baiting of a lion for the amusement of James I.

Alleyn's last performance in the theatre took place on 15th March, 1604. A curious story was told about it at the time. Alleyn was playing Marlowe's Doctor Faustus. Three devils were with him on stage, Lucifer, Beelzebub and Mephostophilis. Even as he talked, there seemed to him to be four devils, not three! Alleyn, it was said, felt intense shock. He believed that the real devil had appeared and was taking part in the performance. This story may, of course, be no more than theatrical gossip but it is certainly true that, although he lived until 1629, he never again acted in the theatre. The stage had lost one of its finest performers.

By the time Alleyn retired from the theatre, he was a wealthy man. He not only owned the Fortune Theatre and the baiting house but also a number of houses and other properties in Southwark. About a year later, he bought the manor of Dulwich, on the outskirts of London. This was a large piece of land which could be used for building. It was the beginning of a venture which greatly occupied Alleyn during the rest of his life. On 17th May, 1613, he signed contracts for the building of a schoolhouse, twelve almshouses and a chapel at Dulwich. He called his foundation 'The College of God's gift at Dulwich'. Poor people and poor scholars were to benefit from the money which Alleyn had made during his successful career in the theatre. When he died, his funeral took place in the chapel at the college and his memorial can still be seen there.

In the Beatitudes, Jesus had said 'Blessed are those who hunger and thirst after righteousness, for they shall be satisfied'. Each age since had

Dulwich College

Alleyn's memorial at Dulwich College

interpreted righteousness in a different way. For St. Simeon Stylites in the sixth century, it meant the single-minded quest for God on the top of a pillar. Righteousness meant having a right relationship with God. For F. H. Lyte in the nineteenth century, on the other hand, righteousness involved carrying out his ministry to the last. He not only preached a sermon but wrote a hymn and a tune. Righteousness meant having a right relationship with his congregation. But the people of Alleyn's time saw righteousness in terms of charity. Lancelot Andrewes' sermon preached at the Spittle described very well the spirit of the age. There were such great inequalities in Elizabethan and Jacobean England. People like Alleyn and the rich merchants of the Port of London were extremely wealthy. Yet there were people who were in danger of starving. Righteousness, at the time, meant getting society right. More schools, almshouses and other charitable institutions were set up out of private funds during that period than at any other time in history.

Understand your work

1 What do you know about playwrights, theatres and actors towards the end of the reign of Elizabeth?

2 Describe the career of Edward Alleyn.

3 What had Alleyn in common with Lancelot Andrewes?

The unknown god

The Piraeus today

The dawn was breaking as the small fishing vessel edged its way into the Piraeus. Paul was among the first to disembark. The captain had already forgotten him, his attention entirely taken up with the problems of selling and delivering fish to the early morning market. Paul set off along the road called Hamaxitos. Even in New Testament times it was an ancient road. His eyes scanned the ruins of the great wall of Pericles and he examined the innumerable altars which had been set up along the roadside. Paul disliked the idea of worshipping many gods. For him, there was only one God. But the altars gave him an idea. He was particularly interested in an altar dedicated to the unknown god.

At last, Paul came to the outskirts of the city. He noticed the cemetery with its many fine sculptured tombstones, then he pushed his way past the busy market stalls selling fish, olives, wine and fruit. It was surprising how early the Athenians went shopping. Paul entered Athens by the Piraeus gate. On his left was the temple of Theseus, restrained and elegant. Then portico after portico caught his eye, painted by famous artists and adorned with noble statues. But Paul was not a man who much admired art. Instead, the tower and water clock of Andronicus interested him, a brilliant device for counting out the hours. Towering over the city, Paul could see the steep heights of the Acropolis.

Paul was not a man to waste time. He began his mission to Athens at the Jewish synagogue. At first he was welcomed. The members of the synagogue were interested in his teachings about a new Jewish religious leader called Jesus of Nazareth. Many of them had heard of him during visits to Jerusalem for the festivals. They only began to object when Paul insisted that Jesus had been condemned to death by the Jews, crucified by the Romans and had then risen from the dead. It proved, so Paul claimed, that Jesus was the messiah, the holy one of God. The Jews could not accept that. They did not expect their messiah to die. They expected him to defeat the enemies of Israel and to rule the world with great glory and power. The Jewish community at Athens began to regard Paul as some sort of crank.

So Paul turned his attention to the Greeks. He began by preaching in the streets, attracting listeners and curious onlookers alike. Athens at that time was full of people interested in ideas, particularly religious ideas. Soon, Paul found himself invited to the Areopagus to argue his case. The Areopagus was a place above the city where trials were conducted and where sometimes public debates were held. The council of the Areopagus wielded great power in first century Greece. If Paul could convince some of its members, it would greatly strengthen his cause.

A view of the Acropolis, showing the Areopagus on the left of the picture

When Paul arrived at the Areopagus, he found a large audience waiting for him. 'Men of Athens,' said Paul, 'I percieve that in every way you are very religious. For as I passed along and observed the objects of your worship, I found also an altar with this inscription, "To the unknown god". What therefore you worship as unknown, I proclaim to you.' The Greeks listened with great interest until Paul started to explain that Jesus had been crucified and had then risen from the dead. Then most of them reacted angrily. Just as the Jews had rejected Paul's teachings, so did the Greeks. To them, a god was perfect and therefore incapable of death. If Jesus was the holy one of God he would certainly not have died. As Paul wrote later to his friends at Corinth, 'we preach Christ crucified, a stumbling block to the Jews and folly to the Gentiles.'

When Paul left Athens, he had little to show for his visit to the city. The Jewish community had thought of God in terms of power. They would not have accepted, either, Jesus' teaching that the kingdom of heaven is for 'the poor in spirit' or that the meek shall inherit the earth. The Greek community, on the other hand, were inclined to think of gods as perfections – perfect beauty, perfect love, perfect skill, perfect strength. So Jesus' humanity and his concern with ordinary people did not fit in with their ideas.

During the long history of Christianity, religious beliefs have taken many forms. The principles were laid down by Jesus in his Beatitudes and they led both to his crucifixion and to the establishment of a great world religion. But the principles have been interpreted in many different ways. The preachers of the Middle Ages, for instance, were not averse to terrifying their congregations with graphic descriptions of great fires, stoked by devils and burning people everlastingly. The idea was to frighten people into goodness. Christopher Marlowe, at least did not believe in such a hell:

> *Faustus* How comes it then that thou art out of hell?
> *Mephostophilis* Why this is hell, nor am I out of it.

That is very near to Jesus' teaching that the kingdom of heaven is a way of life. Marlowe, taught too the endless mercy of God, sending his good angel to Faustus long after he has signed his deadly contract with Mephostophilis. The beliefs of Christianity have, throughout the centuries, greatly affected the lives of people. Perhaps the story about Alleyn and the extra devil on stage is untrue but the fact remains that he did spend large sums of his money on 'The College of God's gift at Dulwich'.

Understand your work

1 What did Paul see when he first visited first-century Athens?

2 Why did the Jews and the Greeks reject Paul's teachings?

3 What was Christopher Marlowe's idea of hell and in what way was his teaching near to the teaching of Jesus?

6 Work Section

Understand your work

1 Who did Ruth mourn and how was she comforted?

2 When did H. F. Lyte believe that he would see God?

3 Describe the discoveries at Nag Hammadi in Egypt.

4 What connections are there between the Beatitudes and other parts of the Bible?

5 Describe Kit Marlowe's reputation in 1601.

6 What was an Elizabethan theatre like?

7 Why were theatres built outside the city walls in Elizabethan London?

8 How did Dulwich College come into existence?

9 Why did Paul visit the Areopagus?

10 Why did Paul take an interest in the altar to the unknown god?

Find out more

1 Read Luke 6, 20–26. This is St. Luke's version of the Beatitudes. Answer the following questions:
   a Which of St. Matthew's Beatitudes are left out here?
   b What is the other main difference between St. Luke's version and St. Matthew's version of the Beatitudes?

2 Religious belief can often be the result of a vision or an intense emotional experience. Read Isaiah 6, 1–8 and answer the following questions:
   a Where was Isaiah when he received his vision?
   b What were the seraphim like?
   c What did they chant to each other?
   d How did Isaiah react to his vision?
   e What did one of the seraphim do in Isaiah's vision?
   f What did Isaiah then say?

3 St. Paul's conversion was a complicated affair. He was an enemy of the early Christians but, in his heart of hearts, he suspected that the very people he was persecuting were right and he was wrong. Then, on the road to Damascus, he had a sudden and dramatic experience. Read Acts 9, 1–19 and answer the following questions:
   a What did the first-century Jews call Christianity?
   b What happened to Saul?
   c Who else received a vision?
   d Why did Ananias hesitate?
   e What did Ananias say to Saul?
   f What did he do?

4 Everything written in the New Testament was produced in order to help people believe in Christianity. Read I John 1, 1–4 and answer the following questions:
   a Jesus here is called 'the word of life'. What does the author say about his contact with Jesus?
   b What does the author mean when he says that 'the life was made manifest'?
   c What is the purpose of his letter?
   d How does Christian fellowship come into it?

5 In the year 731 AD, The Venerable Bede, a monk from Jarrow, completed his book, *A History of the English Church and People*. In it, he tells, among other things, the story of the martyrdom of St. Alban:

> *When these unbelieving Emperors were issuing savage edicts against all Christians, Alban, as yet a pagan, gave shelter to a Christian priest fleeing from his pursuers. And when he observed this man's unbroken activity of prayer and vigil, he was suddenly touched by the grace of God, and began to follow the priest's example of faith and devotion. Gradually instructed by his teaching of faith and salvation, Alban renounced the darkness of idolatry, and sincerely accepted Christ. But when the priest had lived in his house some days, word came to the ears of the evil ruler that Christ's holy confessor, whose time of martyrdom had not yet come, lay hidden in Alban's house. Accordingly he gave orders to his soldiers to make a thorough search, and when they arrived at the martyr's house, holy Alban, wearing the priest's long cloak, at once surrendered himself in place of his guest and teacher, and was led bound before the judge.*

This led to Alban's death in the place of the priest. Answer the following questions:
   a What impressed Alban about the priest staying in his house?
   b Why was the priest in danger?
   c What did Alban do as a result of his contact with the priest?
   d What did the evil ruler hear?
   e What did he do?
   f How did Alban save the priest's life?
   g How does Bede tell us that, at a later date, that priest was also martyred?

6 Christianity has always used symbols, like the cross and the fish, to express the faith. Collect as many such symbols as you can and find out their origins.

7 St. Thomas a Kempis was a German priest who, around the year 1413, wrote one of the most remarkable books in the history of Christainity. It is called *The Imitation of Christ*. In it, he describes Christian thought and behaviour in the light of the life of Jesus:

> *Those to whom the Eternal Word speaks are delivered from uncertainty. From one Word proceed all things, and all things tell of Him; it is He, the*

Author of all things, who speaks to us. Without him no one can understand or judge aright. But the man to whom all things are one, who refers everything to One, and who sees everything as in One, is enabled to remain steadfast in heart, and abide at peace with God.

Answer the following questions:

a Apart from the beginning of sentences, there are several words in this passage beginning with a capital letter where, normally, we would not use one. Can you discover why the author has used these capitals?

b How does the author describe religious inspiration?

c What connection do you see between this passage and the first epistle of John?

d How does St. Thomas a Kempis explain that Jesus is at the centre of all things?

e What are Christians to do if they wish to understand or judge aright?

8 On 14th April, 1925, Herbert Hensley Henson, Bishop of Durham, wrote a letter to a young man who was thinking of becoming a clergyman but who had great doubts about the teachings of the Church. One of the difficulties such people face is that, because the Church has been in existence for nearly two thousand years, a great deal is written in what is now antique language:

My dear Ian,

> *I have read your letter with great interest and sympathy. Indeed I take it as an evidence of genuine friendship that you should write so frankly.*

> *The specific obstacles which you mention do not strike me as quite so formidable and final as you judge them to be. Thus the Trinitarian theology, which has its most elaborate formulation in the so-called Athanasian Creed, is admittedly archaic in form, expressing the truth about the Divine Nature in the terms of the philosophy which generally prevailed in the 4th and 5th centuries. The Church retains these ancient Creeds, not because they are wholly satisfying, but because they express with great dignity, and the large prestige of their antiquity and Catholick authority, truths which we hold to be vital. When we can gain a more satisfactory formulation of what we believe, we may replace the Creeds.*

Answer the following questions:

a Why is the bishop pleased that the young man has written to him frankly?

b What is meant by 'Trinitarian theology'?

c You will find the Athanasian Creed under the title 'At Morning Prayer' in the Book of Common Prayer. When is this creed to be said by members of the Church of England?

d How does the bishop explain why the Church keeps ancient creeds like this?

e Does he think there is any way in which they might be replaced?

9

Answer the following questions:

a Why does Woody Allen say that God is silent?

b How does Woody Allen suggest that talking about religion does not always help religious belief?

10 Because the Church is very ancient and develops very slowly, some Christians have been inclined to think that it is very stuffy. Here is a poem by T. S. Eliot:

The broad-backed hippopotamus
Rests on its belly in the mud;
Although he seems to firm to us
He is merely flesh and blood.

Flesh and blood is weak and frail,
Susceptible to nervous shock;
While the True Church can never fail
For it is based upon a rock.

The hippo's feeble steps may err
In compassing material ends,
While the True Church need never stir
To gather in its dividends.

Answer the following questions:

a Read Matthew 16, 18. Why does Eliot say that the True Church is based on a rock?

b How does he refer to the money invested by the Church?

Acknowledgements

The publishers would like to thank the following for permission to reproduce photographs:

Reverend Allen, pp. 38, 56, 57, 60, 70: A. Anholt-White, pp. 46, 47, 58, 70; Bodleian Library, pp. 59, 63, 65; W. Braun/ZEFA, p. 18; Nicholas Brazil, p. 51; Bridgeman Art Library, p. 74; Cambridge University Library, p. 61; Camera Press, p. 25; Dr. James Stevens Curl, p. 35; Glasgow University Library, p. 62; Sally and Richard Greenhill, pp. 22, 24, 25; Sonia Halliday, p. 71; André Held/Ziolo, p. 48; Michael Holford, pp. 4, 60; IBM U.K. Ltd., p. 63; John and Mary Kent, p. 36; Mansell Collection, pp. 12, 46; Musée du Louvre, pp. 21, 36; Museum of Science and Industry, pp. 62, 63; National Portrait Gallery, London, p. 26; Picturepoint, p. 61; Popperfoto Ltd., pp. 14, 15; Alan Richards, p. 39; Ronald Sheridan, pp. 4, 55, 60, 76; R. Vanstone/Dulwich College, p. 75; Woodmansterne, p. 59. *Back cover*: Victoria and Albert Museum/Michael Holford.

Illustrations by Arthur Barbosa, John Fraser, Tudor Humphries, John Keay, Chris Molan, Tony Morris. The cover illustration is by Paul Leith. 'The New Jerusalem' on page 39 is by Alan Richards.

Grateful acknowledgement is made for the following:

Franco Nencini *Florence, The Days of the Flood*, London 1967; Thomas Birch *The Court and Times of James I*, London 1848; H.F. Lyte *Remains*, London 1850; *History Today*; *Selected Poems of Gerard Manley Hopkins* London, 1953; *St Cyril of Jerusalem's Lectures on the Christian Sacraments* ed. F.L. Cross, London, 1951; Roger McGough *Three Rusty Nails*; Richard Hughes *Dog at a Catch*, Oxford 1979 (Midday Publications); Marcel Quoist *Prayers of Life*, London 1951; Isaac Watts *Hymns A & M*; Sydney Carter *Songs of Sydney Carter in the Present Tense*, Book 3; Fynn *Mister God this is Anna*, London 1974; A.G. Prys-Jones c.f. *Oxford Book of Welsh Verse*, O.U.P. 1977; C.S. Lewis *The Screwtape Letters*, Geoffrey Bles, 1942; Dylan Thomas *Collected Poems 1934–52*, Dent, 1942; T.J. Morris *A Manual for Communicants*, Church in Wales Publications; The Venerable Bede *A History of the English Church and People*, Penguin 1955; Thomas a Kempis *The Imitation of Christ*, Penguin 1952; The Letters of Herbert Hensley Henson Ed. Evelyn Foley Braley, S.P.C.K. 1954; T.S. Eliot *Collected Poems 1909–1935*, Faber, 1936; A.S. Konisberg *Inside Woody Allen*, London, 1978.

Book List

Where direct quotation of the Bible has been used, the translation is the Revised Standard Version (Oxford University Press). References follow the convention that the first number is a chapter number and the second a verse number.

It is assumed that the school library will already have a suitable concordance and a number of general biblical commentaries, bible atlases and other works which supply background material. The following books, however, would be useful to supplement the usual list:

C.G. Dodd	*The Parables of the Kingdom*, pub. Nisbet and Co. Ltd, London 1935
Philip Gaskell	*A New Introduction to Bibliography*, O.U.P., 1972
A.N. Gilkes	*The Impact of the Dead Sea Scrolls*, Macmillan, 1962
Joachim Jeremias	*The Parables of Jesus*, S.C.M. Press, 1954
	The Christ's Hospital Book, London 1953
John Stow	*Survey of London*, Everyman, 1956